You Asked For It

The moment you saw this book, you were probably thinking "WTF?". Whether it was anger, disgust, intrigue, excitement, or curiosity that caused you to pick up this book and open it is completely irrelevant. You opened it. And you're probably going to tell others about it.

That's what this book is all about. It's about how to leverage the emotions we all have in order to prosper in business and life. Not by exploiting people in a bad way – by exploiting them in a way they desire to be exploited.

If you're a politically correct individual, you should probably put this book down right now, as it might give you a heart attack. If, on the other hand, you want to power-up your marketing and sales skills, becoming ridiculously wealthy, gain a competitive advantage over others, or take control of your emotions, this book is for you.

Profiting From Fear
First Edition

First published September, 2019

Author's Notes:

This book consists of my opinions. As in all things in life, make your own decisions and choose carefully. Unless specifically stated otherwise, names, characters, places, ideas, and events are solely the creation of my creative imagination. Individuals and companies mentioned in this book did not endorse the content or concepts of this book.

Profiting From Fear

Profiting From Fear is...

"Pure gold!

... changes the marketing and self-improvement games forever"

Aiden S.
Entrepreur and author

Other Books In The "Zero To Hero" Series

Other books in the "Zero To Hero" series are listed below. Be sure to visit http://zerotohero.co for updates on new publications.

Perpetual Wealth:
How To Achieve Financial Freedom And Ensure You Never Run Out Of Money

This book changes the game on becoming wealthy. Use the secrets of the ultra-rich to ensure your success, gain freedom from financial slavery, and ensure lifelong prosperity.

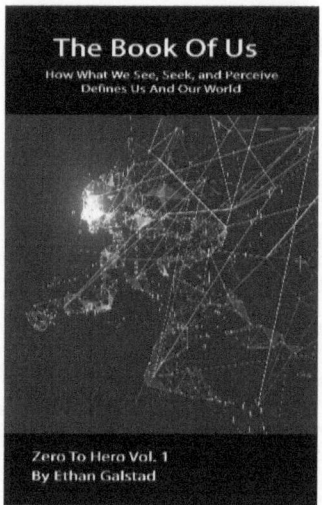

The Book Of Us:
How What We Seek, See and Perceive Defines Us and Our World

This book offers new perspectives on society, belief systems, and relationships.

About This Book

This book is part of a "Black Book" series of financial publications that are intended to empower individuals by increasing their knowledge of finance, investing, wealth, and business, so they can achieve greater levels of success and enjoy life to the fullest.

This book takes an in-depth look at the power of human emotions, the factors that drive decision-making and consumerism, and methods for delivering solutions that your target market craves. It'll show you how to make a killing by selling products and services to people that didn't even think they needed them.

You're not likely to find the information in this book anywhere else. Once you understand the power of being able to exploit emotions for your personal and financial gain, you're never going to let this book go.

Book Updates and Related Video Content

Supplemental content and videos that go into deeper depth on the topics discussed in this book can be found free of charge on the ZeroToHero website at http://zerotohero.co

Additional resources that correspond to the subjects covered in this book can also be found at the website listed above.

Feedback and Suggestions

Have comments, questions, or suggestions for future revisions of this book or for other ideas you'd like to hear about? I'd love to hear from you!

Contact me on the http://zerotohero.co website and I'll get back to you as soon as I can. Thanks!

About The Author

Some of my fondest memories as a child relate to reading my parents' encyclopedia set. I remember spending hours pulling out each volume and reading about different topics. That love for learning remained a core part of me as I grew up. I loved spending hours at the library perusing different sections and would often spend time on the weekends at used bookstores. Some of my favorite types of books were mysteries, as I was always interested in the discovery of something new or the unearthing of something that was lost or forgotten long ago.

My love of discovering the unknown has led me down a path of attempting to connect the dots between separate viewpoints, topics, and scientific fields throughout my life. This drive to discover something new has led me to create what I consider to be new or different viewpoints and concepts than what others have presented.

Regardless of whether you agree with my thoughts on things or not, I have always cherished different and new perspectives on topics, and I hope my writings offer you something new to contemplate.

Best regards,

Ethan Galstad
Author

Foreword

My intention with this book is to help people maximize their success and financial prosperity, as well as their personal understanding and mastery of emotions. I have written this book in a manner that presents complex ideas and systems in an easy to understand format, so as to ensure it is received as well as possible by a large, diverse audience. I welcome any feedback, questions, and criticisms you may have on the ideas I present.

I encourage you to not simply accept what I write as outright facts. Rather, I believe it is in your best interest to seek differing opinions on the topics I present, so you can make your own decisions. Remember... a wise man (or woman) seeks the counsel of multiple perspectives before accepting new ideas or adjusting their worldview.

I rarely ever trust one person's opinion (or one book's ideas or philosophies) before making my own decisions. Seek knowledge from different sources and people and make your own decisions and judgments as to what is the best path for you to follow and what ideologies fit with yours. This is your life, so live it without regret and follow your inner voice and gut feeling always. As they say, to thine own self be true.

Thanks to my mentors, role models, and friends who helped inspire and review this book. And thanks to the Amazon team for building an amazing platform that allows independent-minded thinkers to self-publish books in minimal time. Last but not least, thank you for taking some of your precious time to read my books. I truly hope you find them insightful and helpful in your life.

Profiting From Fear

How To Leverage Emotions, Exploit Weaknesses And Make A Killing

Table of Contents

Section 1 – Introduction

Section 2 – Understanding And Leveraging Fear

Section 3 – States And Feelings

Section 4 – Leveraging Emotions For Massive Profits

Section 5 – Success And Wealth

Section 6 – Resources

Section 1

-

Introduction

Chapter One
Introduction

How Could You?

I understand that this book may not sit well with some people. The title alone will make some outraged. How could someone write a book like this? He's telling people how to leverage other people's emotions for profit?!? This guy must be a real asshole!

Think what you want, but I subscribe to the saying that it's better to be hated for who I am than loved for someone I'm not. I'm writing this book to give you some beneficial truths, regardless of whether or not they're within your comfort zone.

This Is For Real

Like it or not, the fact of the matter is that we are all exploited on a daily basis. Most people don't even realize it. That's why they're not wealthy. They're slaves to the wealthy masters of emotion.

All of mankind is driven by basic emotions. Emotions define who we are and how we feel. They help us connect with each other, they make us feel fulfilled, they tear us apart, and they leave us vulnerable.

Those who understand the power of emotions and how to leverage them can wield an incredible amount of power.

Religious leaders, rulers, and politicians have for centuries used the power of emotions to achieve great accomplishments. The captains of industry are masters at leveraging emotions to promote never-ending consumerism.

That is what this book is about. It's about understanding emotions and how to leverage them to your benefit.

Specifically, it's about leveraging them for your financial benefit. Utilizing the information you find in this book, you can achieve enormous wealth if you choose to do so. You can also us the information to help achieve mastery of your own emotions for personal gain. What you ultimately decide to do with things you learn is up to you.

In this book I'll cover:

- How emotions influence our purchasing decisions
- How companies leverage our emotions for profit
- How you can leverage emotions for maximum profit
- Basic human emotions and the forces behind them
- Examples of products and services you can sell that appeal to people's emotions

Whether you're a skeptic or a believer, I have little doubt you'll find the simple facts laid bare in these chapters to be undeniably true.

Win Friends Later

Dale Carnegie is famous for writing a number of best-selling books on self-improvement. One of his biggest hits is "*How To Win Friends And Influence People*". That book has many valuable truths that can help you succeed in business and life.

No offense to Mr. Carnegie, but if you want to become wealthy, I'd say it's far more important to influence people than it is to win friends. Your friends won't make you rich, but the masses of people you influence can. If you want to be rich, influence first and win friends later.

Now let's get started...

Chapter Two
You've Been Lied To

Before we get started, it's crucial that you understand that you've been lied to about a number of socially accepted "truths".

Much of what you know and think has been spoon fed to you by society. You've eaten the ideas that others have given you, swallowed them whole, and merged them with your subconscious mind. Those ideas and beliefs have shaped your reality, altered your thinking, and influenced your actions.

Like Neo in the movie *The Matrix*, you need to take the red pill and wake the hell up.

Here are a few of the lies and half-truths you've swallowed:

- **Fear is a negative emotion**. As you'll see in the following chapters, our lives are dominated by fear on a daily basis and it can provide enormous benefits to us. Rather than run from fear and cower in its shadow, you should embrace it, understand it, master it, wield it, and profit from it.

- **Don't judge a book by its cover**. We all do just that, so we stop repeating this ridiculous mantra. The title, subtitle, and cover art of a book attract our attention, and motivate us to pick it up, purchase it, and start reading it.

- **Time is money**. Time does not equate to money. You've been sold this lie and been convinced to trade your time and your life for money. As a result, you have become a modern-day slave to money. I cover ways to escape this prison at the end of the book.

- **Money doesn't make you happy**. A lack of money will <u>severely</u> limit your happiness in life. Having money will remove the stupid things you've been worrying about and <u>can</u> bring you happiness in life.

- **Money is the root of all evil**. You've been messed with in a big way here. Someone apparently doesn't want you to pursue wealth and financial freedom. The fact is that money is good in every aspect. I destroy this pervasive and dangerous lie in my book *Perpetual Wealth*.

- **Greed is bad**. We've been taught that being greedy is bad. Yet we all want more time, more love, more sex, more money, and more freedom. We're all greedy bastards and there's nothing wrong with that.

- **The seven deadly sins are bad**. These "sins" are your roadmap to financial success and freedom once you understand how they influence people and how you can wield them. Accepting them, embracing them, and profiting from them will set you free.

Questioning the truths you've been offered by others can set you free in life. Living someone else's lie will hold you back. Think for yourself. Think and grow rich.

Chapter Three
How This Book Works

I've written this book in such a way as to make it easily digestible by a wide range of readers.

The book features a topic flow that allows you to understand emotions from a wide perspective before diving in deep. In this book, I'll provide you with:

- **An overview of words**. How we use them and how we perceive them is centered around emotion. Understanding words and how to use them is key to mastering the art of profiting from emotions.

- **An analysis of the "good" and the "bad"**. Not everything is what it seems. Understanding both sides of the coin gives you better leverage in your mastery of emotions.

- **The basics of emotions**. Understanding some basic principals will maximize your effectiveness in your for-profit ventures and personal growth.

- **Examples of how companies use our emotions for profit**. Most people don't realize just how easily we're manipulated into consumerism.

- **An overview of how you can profit from helping others**. You can obtain great wealth by understanding emotions and delivering solutions to willing consumers.

- **An analysis of major emotions**. I'll discuss their positives and negatives, as well as methods for exploiting each emotion for profit.

- **Sample ideas for leveraging emotions**. I'll provide sample book titles and advertising slogans that demonstrate just how easy it is to leverage emotions for profit.

- **Concrete steps for leveraging your knowledge for profit.** You wouldn't be reading this book if you didn't want to profit from emotions, right?

- **Success and wealth tips**. You're likely to be more successful if you use the information in this book to your benefit, so I put together some tips on what to do once you're successful.

Let's get started on the good stuff…

Chapter Four
The Power Of Words

Words Are Misunderstood

Words often get a bad rap. They're misunderstood and misused on a regular basis.

For example, take the word "*exploit*". When you saw that word in the subtitle of this book, you were probably shocked or disgusted. That intentionally provocative use of the word was used in order to get your attention.

We've been conditioned to consider the word "exploit" to be negative. It goes without saying that the exploitation of people for harm and the exploitation of security bugs for hacking is a bad thing. That's not what this book is about.

The word "exploit" simply means to "make full use of and derive benefit from" something. This book will teach you how to exploit (make use of) the emotions that people have in order to profit.

Another word that is often looked down upon is "*weakness*". People think that weakness means that someone or something is inferior in some way. That is not the case.

The word "weakness" means to "lack strength", refers to someone or some thing that is "unable to resist", or something that is regarded to be at a disadvantage of some kind. There is no inferiority in weakness.

Weakness simply provides an opportunity for improvement and to give people what they need to feel better. This book will teach you how to use people's weaknesses to improve their lives and to profit at the same time.

Words Are Powerless

Words in and of themselves have no power over us. It is only through our interpretation and response to words, that they have power in our lives.

Many people let words trap them in or move them to a specific emotional state. If you can understand this fact and learn how to master your use of words, you can be extremely successful.

Words Are Powerful

Words can have an immense impact on the way we think, how we feel, and the actions we take.

If you can learn to understand the common emotions that are evoked from specific words and phrases, you have the ability to succeed at levels far greater than those around you.

This book will teach you how to use words to appeal to emotions for the purpose of accomplishing specific goals. It will teach you how to use words to help you reach your personal goals and increase your financial prosperity.

It's How Words Are Used

The power of words comes from:

- How they're used
- How they're interpreted

It's not what you say, it's how you say it. It's the delivery and the context in which words are used that's important.

It's not what is said to you that matters, it's how you feel when things are said to you. It's the interpretation of words that makes all the difference.

Bad Words

We've been told that there are bad words that we shouldn't use. We've been taught from a young age by our parents, our teachers, and society that we shouldn't say certain things. We've been brainwashed. It's not the words in and of themselves that are bad - it's how they're used and interpreted.

The word "*fuck*" is one of those "bad" words. Why is that word any worse than the word "*love*"? Because someone told us so?

The reality is that "fuck" is one of the most versatile, if not the most versatile, words in the English language.

Consider some of the many ways in which the word "fuck" can be used:

- What the fuck was that?!?
- Fuckin' A man, that was awesome!
- Fuck no, I'm not doing that
- Don't fuck me over on this
- I'd like to fuck him (or her)
- Fuck off
- Fuck you!!!

To add to the complexity of interpretation, consider the nuanced differences between an angry "fuck you" and a silly or cheerful "fuck you". Delivery makes all the difference.

Is "fuck" really a bad word? What makes it so "bad"? Is the word itself really bad? Decide for yourself.

Think For Yourself

If you want to massively succeed in life, you need to strip away the lies you've been told, the stories that no longer fit you, and the useless patterns you've fallen into. Think for yourself and you can prosper. Think and grow rich.

Chapter Five

The Good And The Bad

We've been told that there are good emotions and there are bad emotions. We've been told that we shouldn't feel sad. We've been told we shouldn't get angry. We've been told that fear is dangerous and we've been told that happiness is what we should strive for. We've been told a bunch of bullshit.

The fact is that emotions, in and of themselves, are neither good nor bad. It is not an emotion that is inherently good or bad. Rather, it is the way in which an emotion is processed and the way in which we react to that emotion that matters. It is our reaction to emotion, and our follow-through actions that can be positive or negative.

Let's examine a few emotions to see if they're really "good" or "bad" as we've been told.

Happiness

Being happy is supposedly the ideal emotional state to be in. Everyone strives for more happiness in their life. And yet, (most) people aren't in a state of happiness the majority of the time.

So is happiness really a good emotion?

Most everyone would say yes. Yet emotions are not just good or bad. They are not singularly positive or negative. Happiness has its downsides.

A frequent state of happiness can lead to some negative outcomes, including:

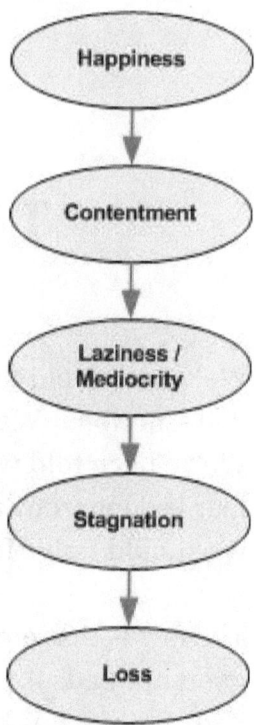

- Complacency
- Mediocrity
- Laziness
- Stagnation

A long-lasting state of happiness can lead a person down a path of self-destruction on several levels if not checked.

Hence, happiness is neither good nor bad. It is how we leverage and respond to happiness that matters most.

Fear

Fear is an extremely powerful emotion. It drives us and influences our thoughts and actions on a daily basis, and yet it is considered to be a negative emotion.

Fear can be an extremely powerful and positive tool if you can wield it. Fear can provide you with:

- Motivation to improve or change
- Self-preservation instincts and actions

If you do not understand fear, or if you fail to control it in your life, it can have a negative impact on you. Fear can leave you immobilized, unable to escape or improve. Fear can leave you feeling defeated and depressed. Fear can destroy you.

Understanding, controlling, and wielding fear is critical to achieving maximum success in life. Use fear, don't let fear use you.

Anger

Anger is said to be a negative emotion that should be avoided. Like fear, anger can destroy you if you do not control it. And yet, anger can also be positive. Anger can lead you to take action, make a change, and improve your life. Anger is neither good nor bad. It is what you do with anger that matters. Use anger, don't let anger use you.

Kinetic Energy

We're told that it's unhealthy (bad) to harbor resentment (anger) and bad to be consumed by fear. Left unchecked, these deep-seeded, powerful emotions can destroy your life. That's true.

I see things from a different angle than others on this. I understand how powerful "bad" emotions can provide massive benefits. Here's how...

When you harbor resentment or are consumed by fear, you are internalizing that emotion in your body. This is akin to constantly charging a battery or storing kinetic energy in a flywheel.

Left unchecked, storing too much energy in a battery or flywheel can cause problems. A battery can leak or short circuit and destroy the thing in which it resides. A flywheel that becomes unstable can come apart violently and destroy the machine in which it resides.

If, however, you utilize that energy in a positive way, you can achieve incredible results. By using the kinetic energy that's stored in your internal battery or flywheel, you have the strength and ability to take massive action in your life.

For example, if you are frustrated (angry) at someone or some situation, you can use that emotion to take action at a massive scale. Your frustration with your weight can make you determined to work off the extra pounds like there's no tomorrow. Your frustration with your job can motivate you to change jobs or switch to a completely different career altogether.

If you are feeling defeated (inadequate), depressed (sad), or scared (fear), you can use the power of those stored emotions to take massive action for change. You can say "hell no, this isn't going to happen to me any more". You can use that stored energy to leap out of the pit you're in and change your life for the better in a massive way.

Although deeply held emotions can be used for positive purposes, care must be used to prevent them from causing self-destruction. There are several techniques outlined later in this book that show you how to help people who are harboring deep-seeded emotions and profit in the process. That is helpful to both them and you.

Chapter Six

The Heartbeat Of Life

We've been told that some emotions are good and some are bad. Some are what we should aspire to feel and some that we should avoid feeling.

There are no such things as bad emotions. There are simply some emotions that are easier to handle than others. It is our ability to understand and control our emotions that matters.

We need the good and the bad, the ups and the downs, and the rollercoaster of a full range of emotions to fully enjoy and appreciate life. We need variety in life or we feel bored – even dead inside.

The whole range of emotions and the ups and downs they provide us are the heartbeat of life. If you stay in any one state permanently, you flat line. Perpetual happiness is not bliss – it's death. There is little enjoyment to life if everything is perfect and there are no challenges to overcome.

It is only through the full range of emotions that we can appreciate life. We need to feel sadness to understand the beauty of happiness. We need to feel the terror of fear to understand the beauty of security and peace.

Understanding that there are no bad emotions is a freeing realization. Understanding that humans need the ups and downs of a range of emotions frees you from the shame of leveraging their emotions for profit.

Money does not reward ideas, hard work, or time. Money rewards value. Thus, in order to profit from people's emotions, you must provide people with value. You do that by helping them achieve their goals. They may want to remain in one emotional state or transition to a different state (emotion) altogether.

It is in that desire to remain in a specific state or in that desire to make a transition that a value proposition is created. That value proposition is your path to profit.

Chapter Seven
Taking Advantage

In order to profit from people's emotions, you need to understand three important things – leverage, value proposition, and expertise.

Leverage

Leverage is simply the process by which you get things done as efficiently as possible. It is the simple machine consisting of a fulcrum and the lever you learned in grade school.

To achieve things efficiently, you can leverage other people's:

- Time
- Skills
- Expertise
- Money
- Emotions
- Desires
- Needs
- Relationships
- Networks
- Property
- Systems

This book is about leveraging other people's emotions for profit. Leveraging something just means to make use of (e.g. exploit) something. We're going to exploit emotions.

Value Propositions

A value proposition allows you the opportunity to sell something to someone for a particular purpose. Value propositions are created when there is a "spread" (difference) between:

- What **they know** vs. what **you know**
- What **they want** vs. what **you have**
- Where **they are now** vs. where **they want to be**
- What **they feel now** vs. how **they want to feel**

For example, if someone is feeling sad now and they want to feel happy, a value proposition is created. If you can provide them something that they think can fulfill that value proposition and get them to a happy state, they'll buy the thing you're selling.

The bigger the value proposition, the greater profit you can generate.

For example, if someone is on the edge of death and they have a desire to live (e.g. not die), a huge value proposition is created. If you have a magic pill that can bring them back from the edge of death, you can charge a hefty price for that pill. They'll pay any amount you charge because the value proposition is immense.

In this way, the more a person wants to remain in a particular emotional state or wants to change their emotional state, the greater opportunity you have to profit. Identifying the biggest emotional drivers in society is your key to making massive profits.

Expertise

If you are selling knowledge, you need to be viewed as an expert. If you're selling a product, the customer needs to believe that your company is a competent leader in the market relating to what you're trying to sell.

Being viewed as an expert (or leader) is critical to selling. Before you start to feel dismayed that you're not an expert, you should understand that you don't need to be a rocket scientist to be an expert. Expertise is relative, not absolute.

If you ask most people whether or not they're an expert on a certain topic, they're bound to say that they're not. What they fail to understand is that they _are_ an expert. In fact, we are all experts on something.

That's because expertise is relative, not absolute. No one person is the utmost expert on any given topic. There are always other people that know something that individual doesn't.

When someone knows something we don't, we think of them as an expert (at some level).

For example, my parents think I'm an expert when it comes to computers. I realize I'm fairly good and that I know more than my parents do, but I know there are experts that know more than me. To my parents, I'm the expert. To me, someone else is the expert. Expertise is relative.

If you are a relative expert (or leader or producer), you have the opportunity to profit by selling something to the consumer that fulfills some or all of the potential value proposition spread.

Using Leverage For Profit And Gain

In order to understand leverage better, let me provide you with a few examples of using leverage for profit.

Mowing The Lawn

If I am getting sick and tired of mowing my lawn, I can hire someone to cut it for me. There are two instances of leverage happening in that scenario:

- The lawn mowing company is leveraging my **need** for my lawn to be mowed and my **desire** for more free time to make a profit.

- I am leveraging my **money** and the lawn mowing company's **time** and **know-how (expertise)** to have more free time for myself.

Notice that there is a bi-directional use of leverage in that example. The exchange of money for services is mutually beneficial. The lawn mowing company profits with money and I profit with free time.

Saving For Retirement

If I am worried about saving money for my retirement, I can buy a book about how to save and invest my money. There are two instances of leverage happening in that scenario:

- The author is leveraging my **fear** of poverty in old age and my **desire** to have a secure retirement, along with their relative **expertise** to sell me a book and make a profit.

- I am leveraging my **money** and the author's relative **expertise** to gain knowledge and relieve my fear.

Again, there is a bi-directional use of leverage that is mutually beneficial. The author profits with money and I profit with knowledge from someone I consider to be a (relative) expert.

Self-Publishing

If I want to publish a book the easy way, I can take the route of self-publishing a book through Amazon. Bi-directional leverage in that scenario happens like this:

- I am leveraging Amazon's **system** (website and publishing platform) and their **customer base** (network and relationships) to publish my book for profit.

- Amazon is leveraging my **desire** to sell a book, my **book** (product), their **system**, and their **customer base** to make a profit off of book sales.

Single Life

If I'm single and I'm searching for my soulmate, I'm on a mission of epic proportions. Anyone that can offer me help is bound to have me as a customer. No one company or individual can find my soulmate (that is the full value proposition) for me – I have to do that on my own.

Although a single company or individual can't fulfill the *full* value proposition of finding my soulmate, they can still help fulfill *part* of the value proposition - each in their own way.

To attempt to achieve the end goal of finding my soulmate, I'm likely to buy services and products from the companies and individuals that I believe are best suited to helping me in that task. Some examples of things I might buy are:

- Self-improvement books
- Relationship books
- Dating site memberships
- Motivational videos
- New clothing
- Gym memberships
- Trips / travel

The list can go on and I'll keep buying if I think it puts me closer to finding my soulmate. The bigger the value proposition, the bigger the profit potential.

For each thing I buy, the bi-directional use of leverage looks something like this:

- The seller is leveraging my **desire** to find someone (or my **fear** of being lonely) to sell me something for financial profit.

- I am leveraging the seller's relative **expertise** or **product** to improve myself and to better my chances of finding my soulmate (my emotional profit).

Both The Exploiter And The Exploited

As you can see from the examples I provided above, we all make use of (e.g. exploit) leverage to profit in one way or another from other people and companies.

As long as we don't intentionally do harm to one another, there is nothing wrong in this dynamic. We are all using each other and being used by each other on a daily basis to accomplish our goals and fulfill our needs and desires.

Leveraging Emotions For Gain

In order to profit in some way, you can leverage people's emotions in the following ways:

- Their desire to remain in a particular emotional state
- Their desire to achieve or transition to a new emotional state that suits their liking
- Their desire to avoid a particular emotional state

For example, if someone is happy and **wants to remain** happy, you can sell them experiences, products, and services intended to keep them happy.

If someone is depressed and **wants to leave** depression for a state of happiness, you can sell them experiences, products, and services intended to help them achieve happiness.

If someone wants to **avoid** feeling fearful or insecure, you can sell them experiences, products, and services intended to increase their feeling of security and courage.

As you see in the examples above, both the seller and the consumer profit from the interaction. The seller receives profit in the form of money, while the consumer receives profit in the form of a specific emotion or feeling. This is a mutually beneficial exchange.

Emotions Trump Logic

Our actions are fueled by emotion. As consumers, we often buy products, services, and experiences based on emotion, rather than logic.

Impulse purchases are a common occurrence for many people. These are primarily driven by our logical thinking (although, sometimes illogical) that the purchase can fulfill an emotional need that we have.

Another example of how emotions trump logic are the studies that show people remember stories, rather than facts. Stories evoke emotions, while facts and logical information do not. Understanding the power of emotions when it comes to consumers making purchasing decision is key when it comes to creating, marketing, and selling a particular service, product, or experience.

Sell The Feeling Not The Product

A common mistake many people make when trying to sell a product, service, or experience is to promote it based on it's features and attributes. This is the equivalent to trying to sell based on logic. While this method can be very effective when someone is looking for a specific solution, it is inferior to selling on emotion.

The key to one's success in a profitable venture is focusing on what a product, service, or experience will provide a consumer to fulfill their need to achieve a particular feeling.

For example, instead of saying that a product utilizes **200 watts of energy** (a logic-based fact), promote it as being "**power-saving**", "**eco-friendly**", or "**green (energy)**". This will appeal to their emotions of wanting to feel helpful, responsible, and cost-conscious (frugal).

Putting It All Together

The bulk of this book is dedicated to providing details on how to leverage specific emotions for profit. With each emotion I cover, I'll provide specific examples of how to phrase titles and slogans that you can use in products, services, and experiences that you sell.

Chapter Eight

How Companies Profit From Our Emotions

Without most people realizing it, their emotions are exploited for commercial gain on a regular basis. There is nothing wrong with that, so long as there is no intentional harm in the exchange. As I've outlined earlier, there is a mutually beneficial use of leverage in each exchange of money for product, service, or experience.

A few examples of how our emotions are leveraged in the sales and marketing process are described below.

Portable Emotions

When Apple released it's first iPod in 2001, it took the world by storm. It was a sexy, sleek new tech gadget that everyone seemed to want. It proved to be a massive commercial success.

Most consumers thought they were buying a portable music player when they purchased an iPod, but there was a whole lot more than gadgetry that appealed to them.

If you examine the Apple marketing posters from that era, you'll see people in a variety of lively poses listening to iPods.

Apple was not selling a portable music player. They were selling you something that appealed to your emotions.

What emotion were they appealing to? Music makes people happy. Apple wasn't selling a portable music player – they were selling **portable happiness**.

They were also appealing to your emotional needs of **superiority** (being the envy of your friends), **uniqueness** (being "different"), **freedom** (the portable aspect of the iPod) and **variety** (the iPod could hold a lot of music).

Winning Friends

Dale Carnegie's book *How To Win Friends And Influence People* has been an enormous success that has helped many people over the years.

The book title appealed to emotion in the following ways:

- The fear of being **lonely** or not being **loved** (the "Win Friends" portion of the title)

- The fear of **insignificance** and not being **successful** (the "Influence People" portion of the title)

- The positive feeling that the reader could reduce their **ignorance** of how to go about winning friends and influencing people (this is the "How To" portion of the title)

- The positive feeling of having some to **trust** who could provide **helpful** information

Making Mad Money That Lasts

My book *Perpetual Wealth* details how people can go about achieving wealth and ensuring they never run out of money in retirement.

The title of the book appeals to a person's emotions in the following ways:

- Their feeling of **lack** in terms of financial stability
- Their **fear of poverty** in retirement
- Their need for **security**, **comfort**, and **prosperity**

Food For Thought

Lean Cuisine has used the phrase "Feed Your Phenomenal" in some of their advertising material. This is a fantastic use of words in marketing and appeals to the following emotions:

- Your need to believe that you are **special** (superior) and **unique**
- Your need for **acknowledgement** of your awesomeness
- The **fear** that failing to continue to consume will put your uniqueness at risk

Clear Service

Tracfone has used the phrase "Get Reliable 4G LTE Service That Keeps You Connected For Less" in some of their ads. The wording of this phrase appeals to your emotions in the following ways:

- Your **fear of loneliness** by losing touch with friends
- Your need to feel **responsible** and **frugal**
- Your need for dependability, reliability, and a sense of **security**

Look And Learn

If you're looking to become successful by selling a product of some kind, it would do you well to consider carefully how to appeal to emotions when it comes to sales and marketing.

Examples of what successful companies do with regards to this are all around you in magazine, online ads, and television commercials. Examine them, dissect them, and duplicate them in your own unique way. Think and grow rich.

Chapter Nine

Providing Value And Helping Others For Profit

Tantamount to profiting from the emotional needs of others is delivering products, services, and experiences that provide value to them.

Money does not reward hard work. It does not reward education, degrees, certifications, experience, or attitude. Money rewards value.

Whether that value is perceived or actual is irrelevant. If someone believes something has value, or the potential of value to them, they will be interested in what you are selling.

This is a vital concept to understand when pursuing any venture with the goal of attaining profit.

You can provide value to others by providing them with (e.g. selling them):

- Your knowledge
- Your services
- Your products
- Experiences

Some examples of things that appeal to emotions that you can sell for profit (or generate profits indirectly from) include:

- Books and blog articles
- Coaching and counseling services
- Seminars
- Tours
- Dining experiences
- Personal services (house cleaning, lawn mowing, etc)
- Clothing
- Tangible products of all many types
- Products and services that make any of the items above easier to sell

As you can see from the list above, anything you can think of can be sold to people's emotion needs for profit. The possibilities for profiting are endless. Anything you can think of can be sold for profit it you know how to sell on emotion. Think and grow rich.

Chapter Ten
Emotional Complexity

Emotions are not as simple to understand as most people think. They are highly complex reactions that are developed over time and based on our past experiences and self-conscious beliefs, rather than just our current experiences and worldview alone.

Although the dissection of the nuances of emotions is beyond the scope of this book, I will describe the basic flow of information that is part of the use and generation of emotions, as well as the outcomes of emotional responses.

Further discussion of these topics will be covered in a future book, but the concepts laid out below should provide you with a basic understanding of the core concepts involved.

If you can learn to analyze emotions and their part in human communication and interaction, you will have a great deal of power when it comes to influencing others, improving your life, and succeeding financially.

Communication And Emotions

Communication lies at the heart of our human existence. Since the dawn of mankind, we have expressed our fears, desires, knowledge, and inspirations through written word, verbal stories, and visual cues.

It is through the various forms of communication that we leverage and develop our emotions. The key to understanding the relationship of communication and emotions is the relationship between the sender/talker/writer and the receiver/listener/reader.

Emotions And The Sender

When we communicate an idea with another person, we are the sender (e.g. the talker or writer). A sender's communication with a recipient is influenced by a complex mix of their subconscious beliefs, past experiences, current emotions and interpretation of the situation or events, their reason or intent for communicating, and the way in which their message is delivered.

When communicating with others, the sender is blending their current emotional states with other factors in an effort to influence the receiver's emotional state in some way.

The diagram on the following page shows the stages a particular idea goes through or is influenced by before it is communicated.

The flow of influence in a sender's communication can be broken down into five distinct parts:

1. **Subconscious beliefs** that unknowingly influence the sender from their past experiences and long-held belief systems.

2. **Past experiences** (recent or old) that the sender knowingly references.

3. The sender's **current emotions and desires**, as well as current events and the sender's interpretation of them.

4. The sender's **intent and reason** for communicating (e.g. to criticize, reprimand, support, comfort, praise, etc)

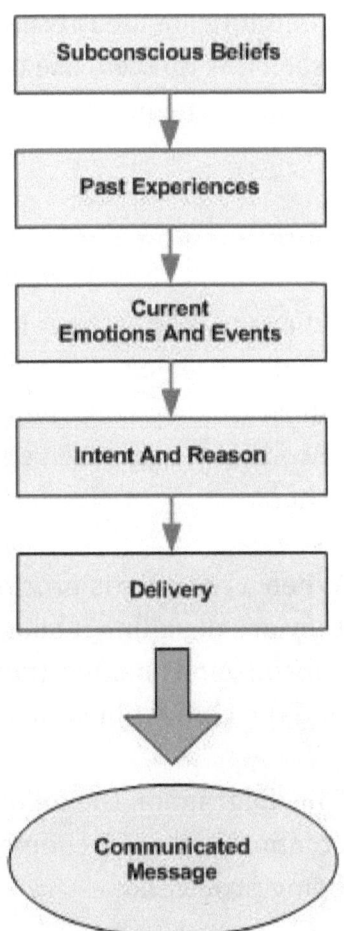

5. The sender's **delivery** of the idea, which includes:

    a. The **words** they use
    b. The **way** in which the words are used (e.g. harsh, demeaning, funny, gentle, etc)
    c. **Physical movement** and **visual cues** accompanying the words (e.g. rolling the eyes, hugging, tilting the head, crossing the hands, etc)

As you can see, communication is a highly complex system that interleaves multiple factors. The use of language to communicate ideas is not limited solely to the words that are used. It is how we use them and our intent behind them that produces the most impact for the receiver.

Emotions And The Receiver

When we read or hear ideas communicated from others, we are the receiver (either the listener or the reader). The way in which we process communication is just as complex as how we encode our intent and emotions in our communication to others.

When a receiver is processing communication from others, they are decoding it using a complex mixture of their subconscious beliefs, their experiences, their current emotions, and the context in which they hear or read the message.

The diagram on the following page shows the complex flow of communication decoding that messages go through before being processed.

The flow that a receiver uses in decoding communication can be broken down into five distinct parts, which are essentially the reverse of what goes on from the sender's point of view:

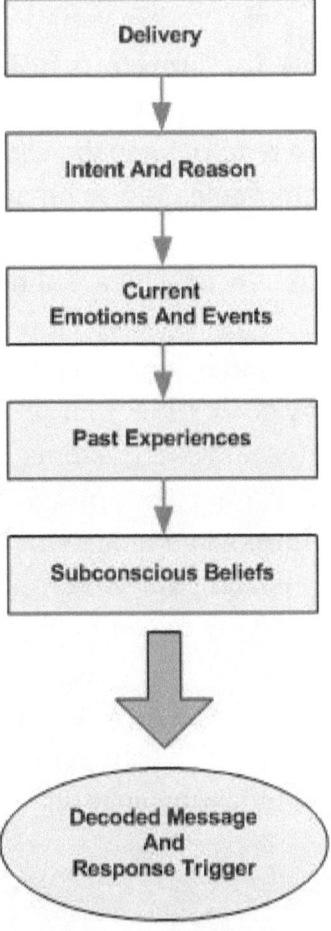

1. The sender's **delivery** of the communication – including words used, the way in which the words are used, and any corresponding visual cues or physical movements that accompany the communication.

2. The **perceived intent** of the sender and their reason for the communication.

3. The receiver's **current emotions and desires**, as well as **current events** and their interpretation of them.

4. **Past experiences** (recent or old) that the receiver knowingly references.

5. **Subconscious beliefs** that unknowingly influence the receiver from their past experiences and long-held belief systems.

As with the sender's outgoing communication, the way in which a receiver processed communication is highly complex.

The interleaving effects of multiple layers of decoding make for an intricate system that can cause the receiver to respond – by emotional, physical, and mental means - in different ways.

The Subconscious Influence Of Response

We tend to view the choice of how to respond to a communication as being determined by our logical mind. However, a significant portion of our responses are driven by our subconscious feelings, needs, and desires.

The underlying reasons we react and think the way we do at any given time is largely driven by the unseen forces of our internal belief systems and subconscious mind. This is one of the primary reasons why it is so important to examine, address, and heal negative emotional barriers from our past. By healing our past wounds, we can react more efficiently and positively to communication from others.

Examples of how people can react to communication, as well as the complex transitions that emotions can take are covered in the following chapter.

Chapter Eleven

Emotional Responses And Transitions

Emotions can be quite complex to analyze. That complexity is magnified when you take into consideration the flows of emotional states and the transitions to other states based on a person's belief systems and the personal choices they make.

You can greatly enhance your ability to influence people and profit if you understand the transitions that are likely to occur between different emotions. To illustrate how to do this, I will provide you with an example of what happens when people are criticized.

No-Bullshit Criticism

For many years, I have considered myself to be a "no bullshit" type of person. By that I mean that I have neither the time nor the inclination to sugarcoat things when I see a need for change in something or someone. I love efficiency and when I see something that is inefficient or that I think will sabotage a goal, I want to fix it in whatever way is most time-efficient.

As such, I have oftentimes been too blunt with people and offered criticism a bit too harshly. While I have always admired the route of gentle corrections that many people opt to use, I usually believe it is best to be straightforward and honest with people with regards to suggestions for improvement.

From my perspective, if something is really bad, it doesn't need to be fixed. Instead, it needs to be "ripped and replaced". That's a simple way of saying that an idea, project, or product needs to be scrapped completely and redone from scratch.

My blunt approach to criticism affects people in different ways, depending on their personality and other factors. Sometimes their responses would be considered positive, other times negative, and sometimes neutral or indifferent.

The impact of criticism on people, as well as their interpretation of and response to it, plays a major role in their outcome.

Consider the diagram below that shows potential outcomes from criticism:

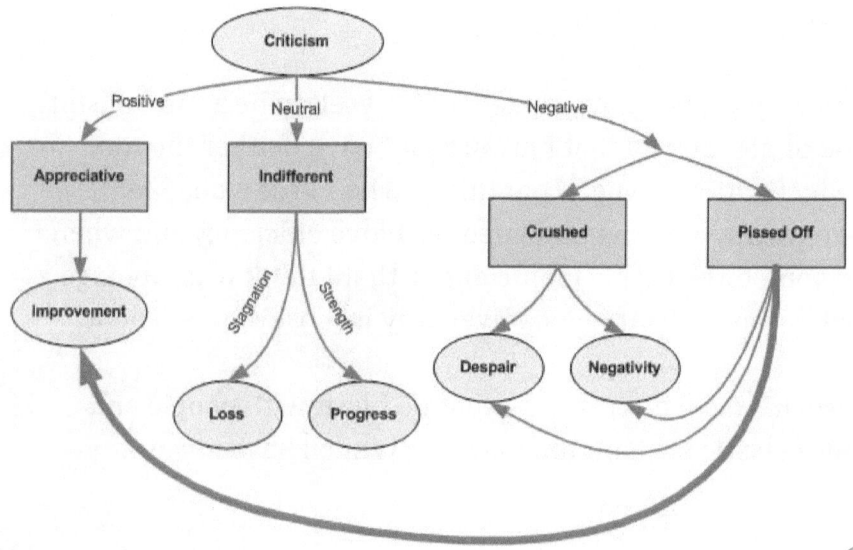

As shown in the diagram on the previous page, there are three main response types to criticism:

- **Positive** reactions allow people to improve themselves and their work because they appreciate the feedback.

- If people are **neutral**, indifferent or uncaring about the criticism, there are generally two things that can happen:

  - If the individual is living a positive life and ignores what they perceive to be negative feedback, they continue on their path of progressing to even more positivity in life.

  - If the individual is uncaring, their skills can deteriorate and they risk losing their job, their relationships, etc.

- **Negative** reactions to criticism can either come in the form of the individual feeling crushed or in them being defensive and pissed off.

Negative To Positive

What is interesting in this dynamic system of emotional transitions is that having a so-called negative response of being pissed off (angry) can actually have the most positive impact on improvement.

While this might seem counterintuitive, people often put in the most effort to improve their life in some way to show or prove the haters, doubters, and criticizers wrong.

I have experienced this phenomenon and I know how positive the outcome can be when I take a so-called negative response and use it as massive motivation to improve in one way or another. As Tony Robbins says, if you want to make a big change, you need to take massive action.

This is a perfect example of not only how emotions are not necessarily positive or negative in a binary sense, but that we are ultimately in control of how we choose to respond to a given situation or emotional trigger. If you take responsibility for and control of your emotions and feelings, you can achieve great things in life.

Profiting From Your Knowledge

Once you understand the different possible outcomes a specific emotional trigger can have on individuals, you can tailor your product or service in such a way as to capitalize on your knowledge. Examples of how to leverage people's interpretation of and reaction to criticism in book titles include:

- *How To Overcome The Haters*
- *F*ck The Critics*
- *Improving Your Life Through Critical Feedback*
- *Show Them Who's Boss*
- *From Crushed To Conqueror*
- *Emotionally Free*

Chapter Twelve
Emotional Perspective

When attempting to appeal to other people's emotions, it is important to understand that people will not have the same emotional response to an event, a slogan, or product offering in the same way.

As the saying goes, beauty lies in the eye of the beholder. What may seem appealing to one person may disgust another person. This concept also applies to emotions. What makes one person happy may make another sad.

Emotional responses – like wealth, expertise, success, and happiness – are relative.

With wealth, someone who has $1,000 in the bank sees someone who has $100,000 in the bank as being wealthy. To the person who has $100,000 in the bank, they view a person who has one million dollars as being wealthy. Wealth is relative. So are emotional responses.

Understanding how different perspectives affect perception and the resulting emotional responses that people might have is key to delivering your message or product in the most effective manner.

An Example In Perspective

To illustrate my point about the relative nature of emotional responses, consider this example: A plaintiff wins a lawsuit against a defendant for $4 million dollars.

In this example, the plaintiff is **happy**, the defendant is **despondent** (sad) and/or **angry**, and the judge and jurors are **indifferent**.

One single event occurred and yet there are three very different emotional responses. The difference in responses is due to the different perspectives the individuals had in relation to the lawsuit.

Art Or Trash?

Graffiti is another example of something that provokes different responses from different people.

When it comes to graffiti, there are several different perspectives and corresponding emotional responses:

- Some people see the graffiti and – thinking it looks trashy – become **angry**, **despondent**, or **disgusted**.

- Some people see the graffiti as being beautiful and clever. They experience emotions of **happiness**, **joy**, and **inspiration**.

- The graffiti artist is **proud** of his or her work and experiences emotions of **happiness** and **fulfillment**.

While the actual graffiti and its placement is the same from the perspective of each person, they each have different emotional responses to it.

Perspectives In Context

The same event, product, wording, or thing will not always provoke the same type of emotional response from the same individual. The emotional response that a person has to something is dependent on their:

- Current emotional state
- Current events around them
- Belief systems and references

To illustrate this point, I offer the following examples:

- While a person may generally think of graffiti as being artful and often experience **happiness** when seeing it, they may not approve of it on historical statues or religious structures and may get **angry** and **disgusted** when they see it in that context.

- While a person may generally be **happy** with their retirement savings, they may become **fearful** if a recession hits or if a recession seems imminent.

- While a person may be **happy** with or **excited** by certain actions in their youth, they may be **disgusted** by or **fearful** of those same actions as they mature.

Quantum Perspectives

The concept of how perspective can change how we view the world around us (and what we think of or feel about it) is grounded in the tenants of quantum physics.

A key component of quantum physics is the understanding that particles, matter, waves, and energy only appear in the way they do based on the intention and belief of the observer. At the quantum level, matter and energy are the same. It is only through the process of trying to observe matter or energy that they materialize into what we're expecting.

This groundbreaking discovery was pioneered by Albert Einstein and his fellow physicists almost a century ago. The implications of these quantum principles are immense and affect everything we know about the world around us.

Various spiritual belief systems talk about us having the ability to manifest, experience, and live in the world of our choosing.

More specifically, these beliefs are based in the understanding that what we see in the world is a reflection of who we are and what our belief systems are.

This viewpoint is one that aligns with the principles of quantum physics. That is to say, what we see and perceive in this world is determined by our belief systems – some of which are taught by society and others that are developed on our own.

If we believe that people are generally good and that the world is a welcoming place, that is what we will notice and experience in life. If, on the other hand, we believe that people are bad and that the world is full of problems, that is what we will notice and experience in life.

Whether we only see or "tune into" things that match our expectations and belief systems, or if the world that each of us experiences is unique to us as individuals, is a debate for the spiritual and scientific experts.

Dr. Deepak Chopra – well-respected author and speaker – talks about these concepts and the interweaving of quantum physics and human experience in his book *Ageless Body, Timeless Mind*. I would highly recommend you read his book if you are interested in such topics.

Chapter Thirteen
Emotional Appeal

In each of the following chapters that covers specific emotions, I'll be discussing the positives and negatives of the emotion, how to leverage it, and concrete examples of book titles and marketing slogans that you use to profit.

Role Reversal

It should be noted that you can approach the process of appealing to a specific positive emotion using three distinct methods:

- Helping them *stay* in a particular emotional state
- Helping them *obtain* a particular emotional state
- Feeding on their fear of *losing* a particular emotional state

You can appeal to specific negative emotions by reversing this methodology. For example, you could feed on their fear of *remaining* in a negative emotional state.

As an example, you can leverage the emotion of happiness in the following ways:

- Appealing to someone's desire to **stay prosperous** with a book title like *Perpetual Wealth*

- Appealing to someone's desire to **become more prosperous** with a book title like *Overnight Millionaire*

- Appealing to someone's **fear of losing prosperity** with a book title like *Ensuring You Don't Run Out Of Money In Retirement*

Each emotion can be approached from a positive or a negative aspect. You can appeal to someone's desire to achieve a particular emotion or their fear of losing or failing to achieve a particular emotion.

Fear Rules

Fear is the predominant emotion that is ever-present in our lives and our way of thinking, as you can fear the loss of every other emotion there is. Fear is the master. Master fear or it will master you.

Section 2

-

Understanding And Leveraging Fear

Chapter Fourteen
Born From Fear

I view fear as being a central motivator for who I have become and what I have achieved in life. I see it as an overriding emotion that is extremely powerful – both positive and negative. I am comfortable with fear and I use it on a regular basis. I leverage fear for motivation.

I have been influenced by the fear of poverty, death, loneliness, failure, success, criticism, inadequacy, insignificance, old age, health problems, loss, abandonment, and shame. We all experience these fears on multiple occasions in our lives and those experiences shape who we are.

As I have learned to understand emotions and use them to my advantage, the way I use my knowledge through words or actions have not always been appreciated by everyone. I've been told that I rule by fear. I've been called a manipulator. I happily agree with those viewpoints and welcome the labels.

Like the word "exploit", the word "manipulate" often has a negative stigma, yet it simply means to control, handle, and influence in a skillful, clever, or unfair manner. I make use of manipulation on a regular basis. So do you.

I am by no means a master of fear - at least in my opinion. I continue to have my own fears on a regular basis and I have to work through them like everyone else. Mastery, like expertise, is relative. So while I may know more about using emotions than others, there are others still that know far more than I.

There are three life-altering instances of overwhelming fear that I experience that have shaped my life and set me on my course. I will share them with you below, so you can more clearly understand ways in which fear has helped you become who you are today.

Hurting Dad

I was bullied by another kid when I was in grade school. A boy had punched and pushed me on several occasions, and I was absolutely terrified of him. I remember running away from him as fast as I could on my way home from school.

At such a young age, I didn't understand why anyone would want to hurt me and I didn't know how to stop the attacks from happening. I was fearful. Terrified.

When my father found out this was happening, he told me I had to learn how to defend myself. I had to learn to stand up for myself and fight back.

I didn't know how to throw a punch, as I had never felt the need to hit anyone, so my father told me that he would teach me. He wanted me to practice on him.

To this day, I can clearly remember him using tape to secure his oversized winter chopper gloves to my little hands. I remember crying when he told me to hit him. I didn't want to hurt my dad. He continued to tell me to hit him until I began to start pounding the gloves softly on his arm.

"Harder! You have to hit me harder!" I was crying, tears streaming down my face, and telling him that I didn't want to hurt him anymore.

He yelled for me to continue and I hit him harder and harder. I was terrified about what I was doing to my dad.

I remember him putting his hands over his head in a protective manner and telling me to hit him on the head as hard as I could. That moment broke me inside and after a few soft hits to my father's head, I was sobbing too much to continue.

That whole experience was so traumatic for me, that I repressed the memory of the entire event for almost forty years. To this day, I cannot remember the bully's name or face, nor what I did to stand up for myself during the next encounter with the bully.

My father has told me that I punched the bully and that he never bullied me again after that point. I don't remember what I did when I faced the terrifying bully. I may have very well beaten him badly because I was so angry at him for having to hit my father in order to learn to defend myself.

Although I have never had to hit anyone else in my life, that event and the fear surrounding it taught me to stand up for myself.

You Will Fail

In 2009, ten years into pouring my heart and soul into a free software project that I loved, a group of competitors and individuals decided to clone my software, attack me publicly, and build their own competing solution using my software as its foundation.

According to them, I wasn't making improvements to my software as quickly as they wanted. Instead of asking me how they could help, they decided to attack me and go their own route.

At that point in time I was self-employed and barely making ends meet. I was giving the software away for free, but was surviving by making some money from advertising on the website and doing some consulting on the side.

My competitors had friends in the media and they attacked me in technical articles that reverberated across publications around the world. One of my big advertising clients decided to drop me and my income dropped substantially.

I didn't have the connections my competitors had and I felt absolutely powerless. I was angry, sad, and terrified about what might happen to me in the future. I was consumed with fears about what my future would look like. I was terrified.

It was at that point that I decided to use my anger and fear to make a stand for myself. I didn't have the connections in the media that my competitors had, but I had a blog. And so I wrote an article that said that 2009 was the "year of the dark horse" and that I was going to come back some day and show my detractors that both I and my project would succeed spectacularly.

Up until that point, I had not released a commercial version of my free software. I had told myself that I didn't want to alienate users who were used to getting everything for free. I had told myself that I wasn't a good enough programmer to develop a commercial version that had substantially improved capabilities. I hadn't had the confidence of belief in myself that I could do it. I had doubted myself.

Because of the enormous fear I felt in 2009, I made the decision that I was going to commercialize my software. I didn't have any money to hire people to help, so I put my headphones on and starting coding like my life depended on it. For the next three months I worked 100-hour weeks and barely ate or showered. I was driven to not only prove my doubters wrong, but to achieve massive success in the process.

I had given myself a three-month deadline to develop the commercial version of my software and I made it happen, just in time. On New Year's Eve 2009 I published the first commercial release of my software. The commercial release of my software proved to be extremely successful and changed my life forever. It allowed me to build what is now a multi-million dollar company with clients across every horizontal and vertical sector. I had succeeded in the face of criticism.

I leveraged the fear of failure, loss, and criticism from that event in 2009 as a motivator to push through seemingly overwhelming challenges and emerge a victor. Fear allowed me to see that I could achieve both personal and financial success beyond my wildest imagination.

Insane In The Membrane

In 2017, just a few weeks before the birth of my son, I experienced a manic/bi-polar episode. I had never experienced anything like that in my life and it was one of the scariest experiences I've ever gone through. The doctors told me afterwards that the stress in my life at that time had caused with to have an acute stress response, which triggered the manic/bi-polar episode.

The scariest part of that episode was when my fiancé took me to the emergency room to get help. From there, I was transferred to a psychiatric wing of the adjacent hospital, where I stayed for several days.

The experience of being in the hospital was absolutely terrifying for me. I was sure that I had died or was lifeless on a gurney somewhere with medics trying to bring me back to life, and was having to live through some after-death type of life review or judgment.

The things I saw and hard – if only in my head – were frightening and life changing. It opened my eyes to the meaning of my life and the people in it.

I was desperate to get out of there and be back with my fiancé for the birth of our son. I remember knowing that my thinking was impaired, as if my brain was half-hobbled or that my internal CPU had overheated. I was terrified that I would not be able to right myself. I knew that the only way I was going to be able to leave was if the staff opened the doors for me and let me out. I had to fix myself for that to happen.

I didn't have many options as to what to do other than think about how to fix myself, so I got to work writing notes and ideas down on paper. I felt as though I had fallen into a deep pit akin to Dante's seven circles of hell. I desperately needed to devise an escape and I knew I had to use the power of leverage to get myself out of that pit of despair.

I'll never be sure what it was that eventually helped me recover, but I remember the feeling of being so relieved and happy when I was able to leave the hospital and return to my fiancé.

The sheer terror that I experienced during that event changed me forever. It taught me the value of leverage, of personal relationships, of the people and connections that helped influence and make me who I was, and of the purpose of my life. I was supposed to help share my knowledge with the world. And thus, I have started writing my ideas in an effort to help people in whatever way – big or small – that I can.

Lasting Effects

We are all forged from fear. The traumatic events in each of our lives leave a lasting impact that determines our mode of thinking and our actions through life. Fear can be a dark master, but it can also be a lifesaver.

Chapter Fifteen

Fear As The Master Emotion

Since the dawn of time, fear has been a powerful influencer in the evolution of mankind. It has shaped our beliefs, influenced our actions, and honed our basic instincts.

How we deal with fear is the determining factor in whether it hurts or helps us.

Reaction Matters

If you were walking alone 10,000 years ago and came face-to-face with a saber-toothed tiger, your heart was struck with fear. How you handled fear had a direct impact on your survival.

If you were **immobilized** by fear, the tiger tore you to shreds. You **died**.

If fear kicked in your "**flight**" response, you ran away and (hopefully) made it to safety. You **survived**. You were **thankful**.

If your "**fight**" response kicked in, you defended yourself from the lion's attack, **survived** and had food for you and your family. You were **thankful**.

If you were **courageous**, you proactively attacked the tiger and killed it. You had food for you and your family. You **made a killing**. You were more **confident** in your abilities. You were **proud**.

Reactions And Results

The diagram below shows different reactions to fear, as well as the resulting outcomes and emotions that result from those reactions.

As shown below, fear is neither negative nor positive. It is only in how we react to and handle fear that matters.

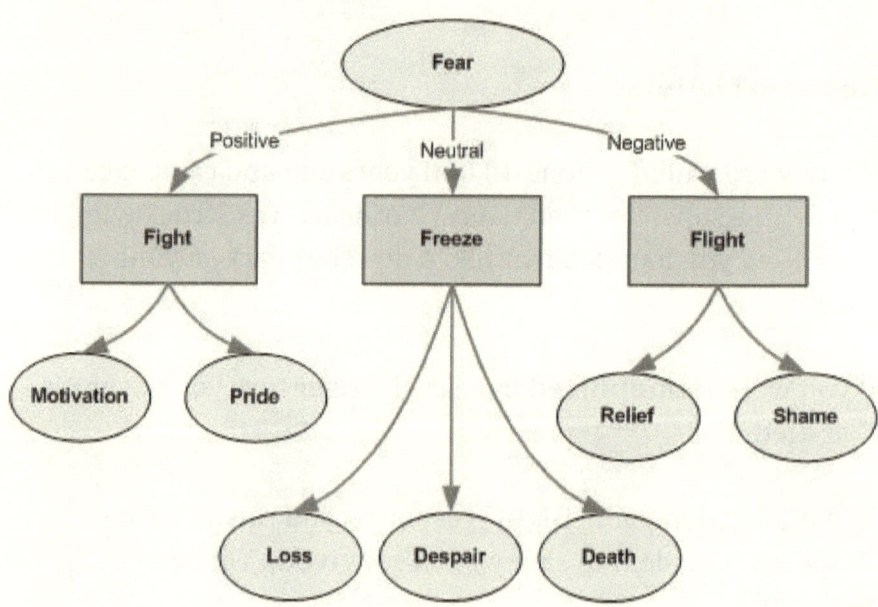

Survive And Thrive

How we handle fear is tantamount to our survival and success in life.

It is when we face our fears that we develop our courage, our stamina, and our determination to continue onwards towards greater achievements. Facing your fears head on requires the greatest courage, yet provides the most fulfilling results.

If you are terrified of public speaking, but keep practicing over and over, you will become more confident in your speaking abilities. As you continue to give speeches, your confidence grows and you aspire to even greater accomplishments. You have conquered your fear and have improved your life.

If you fail to face your fears, it can be detrimental to your growth. If you make excuses about why you can't face your fears, or procrastinate in taking action to conquer them, you should run away. Run as fast as you possibly can.

Massive Success From Massive Fear

If you feel you cannot overcome your fears, you should not stay stagnant or immobilized. You should run. Run as fast as you possibly can. Run like your life depends on it.

Running away can help you survive and thrive. But is in the **how** and the **why** of why you run that determines your ultimate fate.

If you run away from your fears because you do not want to face them, you might be able to avoid their negative aspects, but you will not continue to grow and achieve greater levels of success.

If, instead, you run **towards** your fears like your life depended on it, you can achieve immense success in life. How does this work? Let me explain...

Let's say you have a fear of public speaking. You're terrified of speaking in front of people and have been avoiding speaking opportunities. If you had the opportunity to make $10,000 from a televised speaking event, you would likely turn it down. Even though you'd like to have the money, you'd be too terrified to step up to the plate and give a talk in front of that many people. You'd be terrified of screwing up and looking like a fool. You'd make excuses as to why you couldn't do it.

Your outlook would change if there were a bigger fear in your life than public speaking. If you found out that your son was diagnosed with cancer and his life could only be spared if you had $10,000 to pay for a life-saving operation, you'd be hell bent on saving his life. You'd have massive motivation to do that speaking event. You'd practice speaking like there was no tomorrow and you'd get up on stage even if you were trembling and about to throw up.

You'd make it happen. No bullshit excuses.

The excuses we often make as to why we "can't" face our fears and take massive action to quell them can be overcome so long as we work as if our life (or someone else's) depended on it.

Face your fears and overcome them by **running to them**, rather than away from them.

Profiting From Fear

Profiting from fear is achieved through helping people face and overcome their fears by giving them the tools, information, and courage to become successful.

In doing so, you profit **financially** and through the **satisfaction** in knowing that you've helped others. The consumer profits through greater **confidence** and the ability to **overcome** their fears to achieve greater levels of **success**.

That's a mutually beneficial, bi-directional win for everyone involved. That's beautiful.

The Path Forwards

From here on out I'll be taking you through various emotions and giving examples of how you can profit by helping others. By understanding emotions and what drives people, you can help humanity and achieve great success.

I'll start out by focusing on fear, and it's various forms. Fear, like sex, is an extremely powerful motivator in our lives. The examples I provide will show you exactly how powerful fear is.

I cover many different emotions in this book, and while it is by no means an exhaustive list of all possible emotions, the basics and beyond are covered. You can use the examples I provide in the following chapters to apply the same principles of analysis to any emotion you'd like to profit from.

Let's get started!

Chapter Sixteen

Fear Of Missing Out

The fear of missing out (FOMO) is a perfect example of why fear is not inherently a negative emotion. Fear can be a positive motivator and FOMO is an example of this in action.

The only negative aspect of FOMO is perhaps in the impulsivity it can lead to for consumers. But that's a good thing for the producers of the world and it can help you profit in a big way.

In order to leverage the fear of missing out, focus on making your product or service **scarce** or tie it to something that is **time-sensitive**.

Examples of things that lend themselves to scarcity include:

- Tickets for a concert
- Products on the store shelf
- Passes for a seminar, conference, or event

Examples of things that are time-sensitive include:

- A product promotion
- A concert, conference, or event
- An economic crash that is expected soon
- An investing opportunity that's almost over
- A personal life event like parenthood, marriage, or retirement

Book Titles

Some book titles that capitalize on FOMO include:

- *Preparing For The Coming Collapse*
- *Investing In Bitcoin Before It's Too Late*
- *Preparing For The Birth Of Your Child*
- *Preparing For Retirement*
- *Ten Things You Need To Do Before Getting Married*

Slogans

We've all seen slogans that capitalize on our fear of missing out. Some simple examples include:

- *Limited Time Offer!*

- *Only 10 Seats Remaining!*
- *Registration ends July 10th*
- *Available Only To The First 20 Customers*

FOMO!

As you can see, there's nothing wrong with capitalizing on the fear of missing out.   In the following chapters, I'll demonstrate just how good it can be for everyone involved if you capitalize on all types of fears we face on a regular basis.

Chapter Seventeen
Fear Of Loss

The things we've fought hard for in life and cherish are the things that we fear losing. While deep down we generally understand that we have the ability to rebuild or re-acquire the things we might lose, we are also keenly aware of the amount of effort that was required to achieve or acquire something in the first place. This is one of the main reasons we fear loss.

The fear of loss – in one or more forms – is extremely powerful and is something that can easily be leveraged for profit.

Types Of Loss

There are many things that people fear losing, including:

- Belongings
- Relationships
- Employment
- Opportunities
- Memories
- Computer files
- Money
- Health
- Life

I'll cover recommendations for how to sell based on some of these fears on the following pages.

Loss Keywords

Some general keywords for slogans and book titles that are relevant for fear of loss include:

- *Protect*
- *Defend*
- *Secure*
- *Save*
- *Prevent*
- *Find*
- *Losing*

Loss Of Belongings

We all have stuff in our lives and we all have fears about losing it one way or another.

For example, people have fears that their jewelry may be stolen, their house may burn down, or their phone might be lost.

Here are some book titles that would be applicable to fear of loss of belongings:

- *Protecting Your Valuables From Theft*
- *Flood Protection For Your Home*
- *Proper Storage Of Rare Stamps*
- *Securing Your Home From Burglars*

- *DIY Guide For Home Surveillance Systems*

Loss Of Relationships

Whether it be our
friends, colleagues,
spouse, or partner,
relationships are one
thing that are the
hardest to lose.

A few books titles that appeal to people's fear of losing a
relationship include:

- *Saving Your Marriage*
- *How To Win New Friends*
- *How To Be Your Partner's Best Friend*
- *Date Night Ideas For Struggling Couples*
- *Keys To Preventing Divorce*

Loss Of Employment

At one point in time or
another, chances are we've
all had the fear of losing a
job.

Fear of losing one's job (or
failing in business) can also spark financial fears (fear of
poverty) and fears of failure.

Some relevant book titles appropriate for this include:

- *Preparing For A Layoff*
- *What To Do If You're About To Be Downsized*

- *Being Displaced By Younger Workers*
- *Ways To Improve Your Work Performance*
- *Five Ways To Impress Your Boss*

The latter two examples can also be used to appeal to the positive motivator of self-improvement.

Loss Of Money

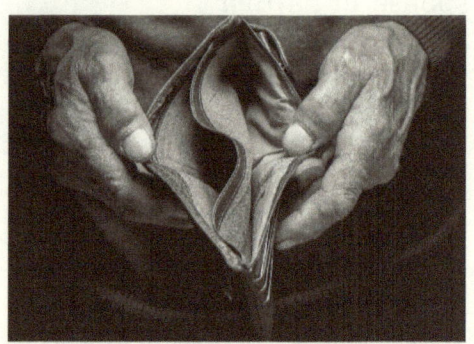

Everyone wants to keep their hard-earned money!

Here are book titles that show ways in which to leverage this fear:

- *Protect Your Bank Account From Hackers*
- *Reducing Risk In Your Investments*
- *Ways To Hide Your Cash From Thieves*

This can also be easily applied to products that are designed to prevent loss of money, including:

- RFID blocking wallets and purses
- Anti-theft backbacks
- Money belts

Loss Of Health And Life

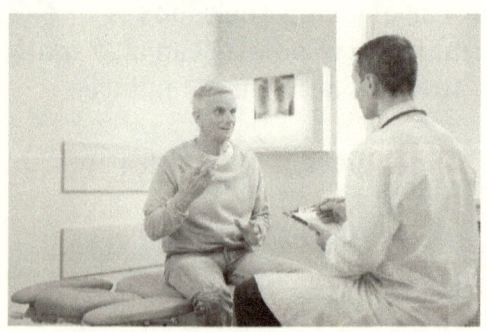

Topics related to this fear can range from anything about nutrition, diet, exercise, and meditation to wills and inheritance.

Sample book titles relevant to the fear of health or life include:

- *Look And Feel Your Best*
- *Achieving Better Nutrition With A Vegan Diet*
- *Simple Meditation Practices For Relieving Stress*
- *Passing On Your Legacy To Your Grandchildren*
- *The Basics Of Writing A Will*
- *How To Beat Cancer*

Chapter Eighteen
Fear Of Failure

No one wants to fail and no one wants to be seen as a failure. The fear of failure is often so great that it keeps people from achieving their dreams.

What most people fail to realize is that failure is how we learn, how we improve, and how we reach our goals in the long run. It is only through trial and error (failure) that the human race has evolved and achieved the tremendous gains that it has.

It does not matter that you fail. Instead, it matters how you respond to failure and what it propels you to do. Use failure as a motivational force to try again and succeed where you first did not. As Will Smith says, fail often, fail forward.

Types Of Failure

There are many things that people fear failing at, including:

- Relationships
- Jobs

- Entrepreneurship
- Presentations
- Finance
- Weight loss
- Parenting

Failure Keywords

Keywords for slogans and book titles that are relevant for fear of failure include:

- *Succeed*
- *Overcome*
- *Courage*
- *Learn*
- *Lost*
- *Fail*

Example Uses

Some example book titles that appeal to people's fear of failure include:

- *Building And Keeping Strong Friendships*
- *Becoming The Most Valuable Employee*
- *Seven Steps To Surefire Career Success*
- *The Entrepreneur's Guide To Success*
- *How To Give A Spectacular Presentation*
- *How To Become A Money Master*
- *Succeed Where Others Fail*
- *How To Be A Great Role Model For Your Children*

Profiting From Failure

As can be seen in the example book titles above, you can profit from fear by helping people overcome their fears. Your ability to do this is often amplified if you can show people how you've overcome the same fears that they have.

When people see that you have the strength and courage to share your fears with others, they become inspired and are more likely to buy what it is that you're selling. This, in turn, helps them to overcome their own fears. It's a win-win scenario for all involved.

Chapter Nineteen

Other Fears

Our lives are dominated by fear of all types. Rather than cover the multitude of fears that exist, I believe you understand from the previous chapters how to go about helping others and profiting from them.

Some of the other types of fears that are commonplace for everyone include fears relating to:

- **Success**. Yes, success. Some people fear being in the spotlight or losing friends when they succeed. Help them with information related to living frugally, humbly, staying grounded in reality, and finding new friends and mentors.

- **Poverty**. This is a fairly common for most everyone. The biggest fears people generally have are related to running out of money in retirement or beforehand. The best ways to profit include helping them invest wisely, save, and practice good money habits.

- **Old Age**. Most people want to remain young. You can use this to market health and exercise tips and products, as well as anti-aging and nutritional supplements.

- **Death**. Focus on helping people with their will, estate planning, passing down heirlooms to heirs, donating to charitable causes, etc. You can also address this with spiritual and religious focused offerings.

- **Loneliness**. While alone time can be great, having someone special in your life is important. You can focus on providing offerings related to dating, love, friends, and social activities.

- **Health Problems**. You can profit from this fear by offering products and services related to nutrition, exercise, vitamins, meditation, natural medicine, yoga, etc.

- **Criticism**. Most people shrivel when they are criticized. You can help them with topics related to improving their self-esteem and confidence.

- **Being Shamed or Humiliated**. Similar to the fear of criticism, but usually in regards to things a person really doesn't want others to know about (e.g. sexual preferences). Shame can also be related to bullying. Focus on helping people with improving their self-esteem and confidence.

- **Being Unappreciated**. Everyone likes to be acknowledged for what they do. Focus on helping people with their self-esteem so they understand what other people do or don't do doesn't matter all that much.

- **Abandonment, Separation, or Rejection**. No one likes being abandoned. Focus on helping people with finding new lovers or friends and boosting their self-esteem and belief in self.

- **Intimacy**. Fear of love and sex. Focus on helping people develop self-confidence and understanding that love and sex are wonderful gifts, even though rejection and loss can be painful.

- **Inadequacy**. Fear of not performing well on the job, in their relationships, in life, or in sex. Focus on helping people with self-help and self-esteem products.

- **The Future**. The unknown is often a cause for concern, whether it relates to the economy, technology, war, etc. Focus on ways to assure people that things will be okay if they have the right outlook and actions.

- **Terrorist Attack**. Although rather infrequent, the nature of terrorist attacks, along with the seemingly random time and place they occur, can cause anxiety. Focus on helping people prepare mentally beforehand and with coping afterwards. Many of the methods of profiting off of economic collapse (see below) also apply here.

- **Economic Collapse.** No one wants to see their economic world crash. You can focus on providing them prepping gear, information on rebuilding after a collapse, and tangible assets (e.g. land, precious metals, firearms). You can also provide helpful information on making their investment portfolio more resistant to downturns.

- **Phobias**. Snakes, spiders, heights, confined spaces, etc. These are often difficult for individuals to overcome. Unless faced with a much greater fear to run from, most people never overcome their phobias.

Fear Rules All

As you can see from the examples I've given, fear is an overriding emotion that drives our lives. Where it takes us is determined not by the emotion itself or the environment in which it is born, but rather by our choice in how we process and react to it.

Fear can kill us or fear can fuel us. It can tear us down or motivate us to improve our lives. The choice is ours and ours alone.

You can profit financially from other people's fears by helping them work through and overcoming their fears. You can profit for yourself by working through your fears and improving your life.

Master fear, don't let fear master you.

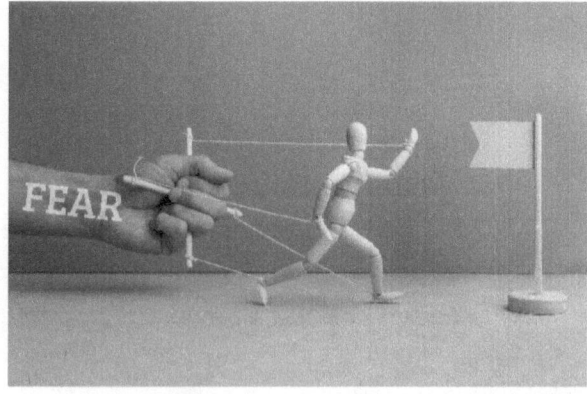

Section 5

-

States And Feelings

Chapter Twenty
Lack

Lack is often viewed as being a negative state or feeling. It is the feeling we have when we haven't yet achieved or haven't yet acquired the things we desire.

Spiritual views on the law of attraction profess that lack can hold us back from achieving our dreams and acquiring the things we want in life. While it is true that a persistent feeling of lack can hold us back, leveraging the positive aspects of lack can propel us to success.

Leveraging The Positive

Fear can leave us immobilized and hold us back in life if we let it control us. And yet, fear can propel us to great success if we leverage its power.

Likewise, lack can either hold you back or propel you to greater success. The choice is yours. If you have a persistent focus on lack, it can leave you feeling depressed and hopeless. Yet, if you leverage lack properly, you can use it to your benefit.

If you view lack as the starting line on a racetrack, and the racetrack as being the race you must run to achieve your goals, you can propel yourself forward in your goal of achieving what you want. Use lack to your advantage. Master lack, don't let lack master you.

Profiting From Lack

In order to profit financially from people's feeling of lack, you must appeal to their sense or need of wanting to overcome that lack.

Here are some examples of book titles that appeal to the feeling of lack:

- *How To Find Your Soulmate*
- *Become A Millionaire In One Year*
- *How To Win Friends And Influence People*
- *Health Rejuvenation Through Meditation*

Note that each of these books both appeals to a person's feeling of lack and deals with a subject that can propel them to greater levels of success. This is the point of profiting from emotions. Help others profit and you will profit as well.

Chapter Twenty One
Greed

In the movie *Wall* Street, Gordon Gecko proudly made the bold statement of "Greed Is Good". This phrase has often been used as a war cry against monetary gain by those who hold capitalism and free markets in contempt. Indeed, most people hold the belief that greed is bad.

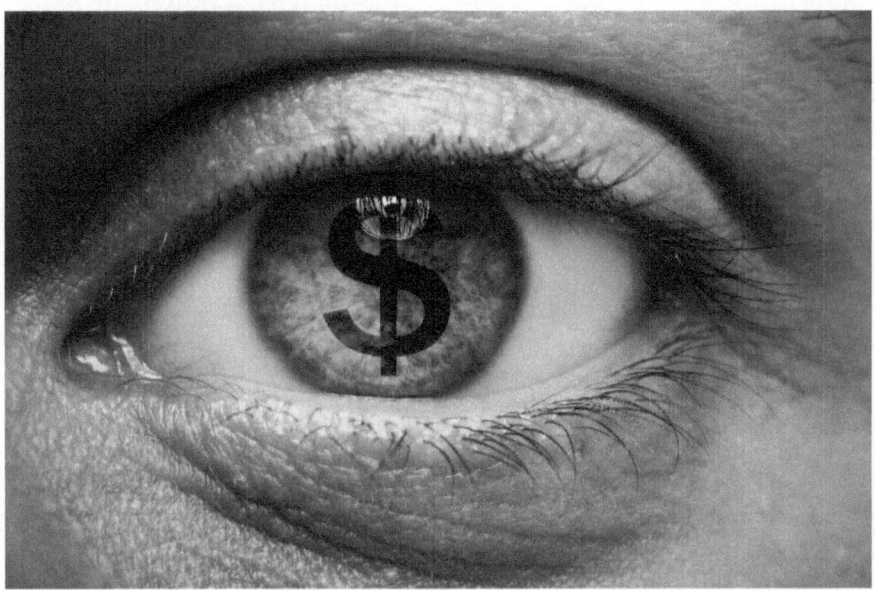

Like other emotions and feelings, greed is neither good nor bad. And like it or not, we are all greedy bastards. We all want more money, more love, more success, more time, more vacation, more gadgets, more spiritual enlightenment, and more enjoyment. We're all greedy.

Greed in and of itself is not bad. Greed can only be construed as bad if we hurt others or do bad things in an attempt to fulfill our greed. In that case, however, it is not greed that is itself bad. The person who is seeking to fulfill their greed is responsible for their bad actions.

The Positive

Like fear, greed can be positive. Greed can be utilized as a motivational force to help achieve our goals or acquire the things we want in live. The desire for something we do not yet have, but which we want, can provide us with a powerful catapult to achievement.

Profiting From Greed

People who are "greedy" want more (often a lot more) of something and they want it as quickly as possible. They also tend to want to acquire something that others cannot – at least to the level or amount that they do. You can leverage this knowledge to create products and services that appeal to these needs and desires.

Some examples of book titles that would appeal to greedy people include:

- *Become A Self-Made Bitcoin Billionaire*
- *Fat To Slim In Just 30 Days*
- *Supercharge Your Earning Skills*
- *How To Become The Life Of The Party*

- *Achieve The Success Others Only Dream About*
- *Experience The World Through Travel Like Few Do*

You can see from these book titles that greed isn't bad. Instead, it shows that we're all greedy in different ways and that greed can catapult us to greater levels of experiences, achievement, and success in life.

So the saying *is* true. Greed *is* good.

Chapter Twenty Two
Denial

When we're faced with facts that don't fit well with our current worldview and psyche, we turn to denial. Denial is neither positive nor negative, but denying problems or shortcomings in your life can hold you back from achieving greater levels of success.

Profiting From Denial

Leveraging someone's sense of denial for profit can be fairly difficult, as their denial often prevents them from reading, using, purchasing, or doing the thing that could prove them wrong.

No one likes to be wrong, so overcoming someone's denial is not an easy task. However, crafty book titles and advertising slogans can be designed to pique a denier's curiosity.

Some book titles and slogans that appeal to people's sense of denial include:

- *The Scientific Proof Behind Probiotics*
- *The Undeniable Proof That Aliens Exist*
- *Find Out Why Everyone's Talking About This*

Ultimately, denial is a sign of a mind that is closed off to possibilities and change. Thus, slogans and titles that relate to proving new things true or expanding possibilities can be quite effective.

The key to profiting from a person's denial is to use wording that almost taunts them to prove themselves right, or provokes their curiosity to see what others are saying about something. Doing this can provoke a strong response that causes deniers to do something or learn something that can benefit them in the long run.

Chapter Twenty Three
Guilt

We've all said or done things we aren't proud of. It is a timeless tenant of the human experience to make mistakes and do or say things that we later regret. When we focus on regret and let it grow in power, we develop feelings of guilt.

Guilt can be a debilitating feeling. It can hold us back from improving our lives and it can rear its ugly head on multiple occasions during our lives. It can haunt our dreams and torment our moments of quiet solitude.

Guilt is a powerful store of kinetic energy. If you let it grow in power over time, it can wreck elements of your psyche. Yet at the same time, the power of guilt can be harnessed for good.

The positive aspects of guilt come from the motivational forces it provide to propel to help you "right" your "wrongs" and change your life for the better. Guilt can offer us a powerful method of developing the courage to overcome.

Profiting From Guilt

In order to profit economically from people's feelings of guilt, you can offer them self-help and self-improvement products and services that appeal to their need of overcoming their feelings of guilt.

Examples of book titles that fit these criteria include:

- *Healing Wounds From The Past*
- *Repairing Failed Relationships*
- *Forgive And Forget*
- *Learning From Your Past Mistakes*

Chapter Twenty Four
Regret

Regret is not nearly as powerful as guilt. Guilt is regret on overdrive. Regret can haunt us for short or long periods of time – depending on what type of regret we have and what it pertains to.

Examples of some types of regret include:

- Not calling your family members often enough before they pass away
- Not spending enough quality time with your children
- Not taking the job you were interested in

- Not taking advantage of travel opportunities
- Not talking to or asking out the guy or girl you were attracted to
- Not paying better attention to your health

Profiting From Regret

As regret is an emotion of lesser intensity than guilt, you can use many of the same tactics as you can with guilt in order to profit.

The key to targeting people's feelings of regret is to focus on ways to help people realize that they have the opportunity to change their lives and do things differently to have a more positive outcome than what they've previously experienced.

Some book titles that serve this purpose include:

- *Live Your Life Without Regrets*
- *10 Places To Travel To Before You Die*
- *Making Your Bucket List*
- *The World Is Yours If You Want It*

Chapter Twenty Five
Other Emotions And Feelings

We humans are extremely complex beings. The multitude of emotions that we feel, generate, project, and communicate offer a plethora of opportunities for improvement and profit. There are dozens of other emotions that have not been covered in this book that can be capitalized upon.

By now you should have a good grasp on the basic concepts of how to leverage emotions for personal and financial profit. I will leave it as an exercise to you, the reader, to analyze other emotions and form a game plan for capitalizing upon your knowledge.

Some emotions and feelings that offer powerful profit potential for you to investigate include:

- Doubt
- Suspicion
- Curiosity
- Love
- Hate

By mastering and leveraging your knowledge of these and other emotions, you can profit greatly in your life. I wish you prosperity in your endeavors with this!

Section 4

-

Leveraging Emotions For Massive Profits

Chapter Twenty Six

Using Your Knowledge To Create Value

Now that you understand the power of emotions and how they can be leveraged for profit, you have to decide what to do next. There are four easy steps for making money with your knowledge:

1. Come up with an idea for a product or service
2. Create that product or service
3. Sell the product or service
4. Profit

Idea Creation And Value Proposition

The first step in making money for your knowledge is to come up with an idea for something you can sell. The process for doing this using emotions as leverage is easy:

1. Pick something that people desire, fear, or love
2. Figure our your angle on creating a product they'd want
3. Create value for the consumer

For example, if people fear running out of money in retirement (which they do), write a book on saving for retirement that reduces their fear, instills them with confidence, and provides them with value.

The bigger a fear and the more people that have that fear, the bigger the market for profit. If you know what people fear, you can profit massively by helping them with their fear.

Likewise, if you know what people love, you can profit by helping them achieve or gain more love.

Types Of Products

What exactly is a product anyway? A product can come in two forms - tangible or intangible.

Tangible products are things that you can touch and feel. Intangible products are digital products and things like copyrights and trademarks.

Physical products are typically more time-intensive in their development process, require warehousing and shipping, and usually offer lower profit margins than intangible products.

Intangible products are ideal for new entrepreneurs to create and are the most efficient money-makers out there. Examples of intangible products include:

- E-Books
- Video and audio content
- Blogs
- Seminars
- Software

I would encourage you to pursue the creation of intangible products and services for profiting from your knowledge.

Write Books

Writing a book – whether it be a long one or a short one – is one of the easiest method of creating an intangible product. Providing your knowledge to others through a book not only brings in money for yourself, but it provides valuable educational material for those looking to improve their lives.

Amazon.com offers authors an easy and free method of delivering their books to consumers – either in the form of digital Kindle books or physical paperback books. You can leverage Amazon to do all the heavy work of order taking, publication, warehousing, and shipping for you. They have an amazing system that is extremely powerful for you to leverage!

Minimum Viable Product

Most people get hung up on perfection. They'll spend countless hours trying to get something perfect and postpone releasing a product or service until they think it's absolutely perfect.

There's no such thing as absolute perfection. Like expertise, perfection is relative. There's always room for improvement, but you can't wait your entire lifetime before releasing something. If you wait too long to get your creation out there, you'll miss the opportunity to capitalize on it.

The key to not getting stuck in a loop of perpetual work on a project is to stick to the basics. You want to make sure whatever it is that you're creating has value to consumers and is "good enough" to release. This is the concept of the Minimal Viable Product (MVP).

Using the MVP concept when you're creating something keeps you on task and forces you to move on once a project has reached its "good enough" point.

I could have taken months to write and review this book, yet I pushed through and did it inside of two weeks. Why? It needed to be published ASAP.

I realize I'm not the best writer in the world and I know there are improvements I could make to this book if I were to take more time. But releasing it in a short amount of time allowed me to move on to my next project – another book and more educational videos.

There's always room for improvement in life, but its best to leave improvements for future releases and future creations. If I focused on absolute perfection, any project I worked on would take way too long to release.

You need to get your idea out there as soon as it's viable and improve it as you go. Whether it's your writing, your videos, your services, it doesn't matter. Get it out there and start improving it once it's released. Use customer feedback and reviews to improve things over time.

Do It Efficiently

There are efficient ways of doing things and inefficient ways of doing the same things. Making money is no different. When it comes to profiting from your ideas, you want to be as time efficient as possible.

I'll cover methods of doing that in the following chapter.

Chapter Twenty Seven
Maximum Efficiency Offerings

Money doesn't reward hard work. It doesn't reward degrees, experience, or the time you put into making it. Money rewards value.

The Value Of Your Life

Most people trade their time for money. They spend most of their adult life slaving away at a job they don't like. They work harder to earn money and then use their money buy bigger houses, increasingly expensive clothes, and flashier vehicles. They're then forced to work harder to earn more money in an ever-increasing cycle. This never ends. They're modern-day slaves to money who are forced to trade their time for more money.

When you trade time for money, you're trading your life. There are only so many hours in the day, so each hour you spend working for money takes away from other more fulfilling ways you could spend your time.

Your life is worth far more than money, so stop trading so much of it away.

Efficient Use Of Time

Rather than trade your precious time for each dollar your earn, it is important to separate your time from the money you earn if you want to increase your income efficiently.

When you earn $40 per hour for each hour you work, you are limited as to how much total income you can generate. When you separate how much money you earn from the amount of time you work, there is no limit to the income you can generate. Instead, you have a potential for unlimited return. That is efficient.

How can you increase your income? Simple. Money rewards value.

The amount of value you provide someone determines how much they're willing to pay you. If you provide little value, they're likely to pay you a little money, if any at all. If you provide enormous value, they're likely to pay you a lot of money.

What you're looking for is maximum income from minimal time. Making that happen requires maximum efficiency. Making that happen requires leverage. Making that happen requires planning and effort. Nothing in life is free. Everything takes effort. But some things come easier if you work smarter.

They key to creating high levels of income efficiently requires:

- **High value proposition**
- **Leverage**
- **Time value separation**

Let's talk about what those mean.

A **value proposition** is created when you know, have, or provide something that someone else needs or wants. When they want something you can provide, there exists a value proposition you can exploit to your benefit. The higher the value proposition and the higher the desire or need, the higher the potential for income.

Leverage involves using other people's money, knowledge, resources, systems, or emotions to accomplish something easier than it would be to do without.

Time value separation means that your income generating potential is not directly related to the amount of time you put into creating whatever it is that you are providing.

Here's an example of a money making machine that meets these criteria...

Writing A Book

Yes, writing a book. Writing a book is one method that can increase your income dramatically in an efficient manner. When you write a book:

- **You exploit a value proposition**. You write about something that you know more about than other people. You don't need to be the world's utmost expert on a subject – you just need to know more than some other people. Since the people that know less about your topic want to know what you know, they're likely to buy your book if they know about it.

- **You use leverage**. You're leveraging what you've learned from others when you write your book. You're leveraging a publisher and/or a publishing platform (like Amazon.com) to get your book out to the public.

- **You separate your time from the value created**. Writing a book will take time, but it will only take a certain number of hours. The number of books you can sell and the amount of income you can generate from the book is not directly tied to the time you put in. This allows for the possibility of an infinite return.

When I suggest writing a book to most people as a way to increase their income, I usually get a bunch of excuses as to why the can't. They say they're not an author, they're not an expert, and they don't have the time. These are all bullshit excuses and lies they tell themselves and others that ultimately hold them back from becoming wealthy.

Everyone is an author. Everyone writes emails and communicates to others via speech on a daily basis. You're already an author. You just probably haven't published a book yet.

Everyone has the same amount of time in the day. How you choose to spend it is up to you. If you want to become financially free and build massive wealth, you have to put in the time. You have to work after everyone else goes to sleep. You have to work early in the morning. You have to work on the weekends. There is no gain without pain.

Everyone is an expert on something because expertise is relative, not absolute. You may not be the world's utmost expert on any given topic, but you know more about it than some other people.

If you write about a topic that people are interested in, the people who know less about it than you do are your target market. You are a relative expert on the subject compared to them.

When it comes to choosing a title for your book, you need to leverage and exploit other people's emotions and basic desires.

For example, everyone generally wants more money, more time, more success, and more love. And we want it easier, faster, cheaper, and better. We're all greedy bastards.

Example book titles that exploit these desires and leverage emotions include:

- *10 Easy Ways For Single Moms To Make More Money*
- *How To Be A Successful Entrepreneur*
- *How To Build A Secure Retirement Nest Egg*
- *Find Your Soulmate In Five Simple Steps*
- *Get Rich And Live The Life You've Dreamed Of*
- *The 4-Hour Work Week*
- *The Millionaire Next Door*
- *Think and Grow Rich*

Those are titles that exploit the desires and emotions of other people. There's nothing wrong with that. That's just how you get things done effectively and efficiently.

Other Options

Writing a book isn't the only efficient method of increasing your income. Here are a few other ways you can accomplish the same goal:

- Produce videos on YouTube and monetize the channel
- Write a software application
- Build a tutorial series
- Run a seminar or conference

All of those options have the same three attributes:

- Value proposition
- Leverage
- Time value separation

Get To Work

You can either make excuses or you can make more money. You can't do both. If you want to be financially free and build lasting wealth, you have to make the effort. No one is going to do the work for you. You have to do it. So if you decide more money is what you want, stop making excuses and get to work.

Chapter Twenty Eight
Winning Combinations

A powerful double-whammy of marketing genius can be created by following some of the simple ideas outlined below.

Saving Time

People often feel overwhelmed and are looking for ways to save time so they can relax. Using this knowledge, you can craft slogans and book titles that appeal to a person's need for time along with their emotional needs.

You can leverage lack of time in combination with other emotional needs with book titles like this:

- *Five Easy Steps To Success*
- *The Fast Millionaire Method*
- *Quick Ways To Overcome Phobias*
- *Get A Raise In No Time Flat*
- *Easy-Peasy Ways To Make Extra Money*

The words "easy", "fast", "quick", and the phrases "no time" and "easy-peasy" indicate that a task or job doesn't take much time. When people are pressed for time (which is often the case), they're looking for things that can be done quickly. If you can appeal to that need, you've upped your chances of success.

Where There's A Will There's A Way

Aside from time, people often feel a lack of willpower. If they just took action, the wouldn't feel that way, but it's human nature to sit back and feel like you don't have the will to accomplish a certain task. You can leverage this lack of willpower with book titles such as:

- *Finding The Courage To Succeed*
- *Discipline Your Mind, Body, and Spirit*
- *Making Success Happen Come Hell Or High Water*
- *Don't Stop Achieving Greatness*
- *Winners Take All*

Dual Hitter

Combining two or more emotional appeals in a book title or marketing slogan can increase your chances of success.

For example, the book title ***Finding Success And Happiness In Life*** appeals to two emotional needs – **success** and **happiness**.

Specifically, the title appeals to the feeling of lacking these emotions, as the word "finding" implies the reader doesn't have either of these in his or her life (to the level they want) at the present time.

Chapter Twenty Nine
Advanced Topics

Now that you've read this book, you understand the power of emotions and know the basics of how to leverage them for profit.

While powerful in their own right, using emotions to your benefit is just the beginning. Emotions are the baby steps in understanding how to profit from people. But there's something even more powerful and profitable to leverage – desires and basic instincts.

Desires are at the core of our human instinct. They drive our emotions and actions.

When we think we're controlling ourselves because we have our emotions in check, we're not. Desires are the primordial engines under the hood that influence our thoughts, judgments, emotions, and actions.

If you're ready to unleash the explosive power of desires and profit like there's no tomorrow, you need to understand the desires that drive people, how to fulfill those desires, and how to keep people coming back to you for more.

If you can master desires, you'll have people begging you at your doorstep (or storefront) for more. People need to have their desires filled and you can profit immensely by giving them what they want.

Sell Them Sex

If you thought the title of this book was controversial, you'll probably flip your lid when you see my upcoming book.

I've outlined the secrets of profiting from desires in my upcoming book – *Sell Them Sex: How To Exploit Desires And Entice Customers For Maximum Profit.*

The title, subtitle, and cover are intentionally meant to be provocative.

In *Sell Them Sex*, I teach you how to understand and master desires, wants, and primal urges for maximum profit. I show how the "Seven Deadly Sins" are your roadmap to financial success.

Sex sells. Big time. If you want to create massive wealth faster than you ever thought possible, *Sell Them Sex* is a must read.

Sell Them Sex is scheduled for release in October of 2019.

The Dirty Secrets You Were Never Taught

SELL
THEM
SEX

How To
Exploit Desires
And Entice Customers
For Maximum Profit

Zero To Hero
Financial Black Book Series
By Ethan Galstad

Scheduled for release in October of 2019

Section 5

-

Success And Wealth

Includes excerpts from my book

Perpetual Wealth

Chapter Thirty
Always Be Hungry

The masses of people live mediocre lives. They achieve a certain level of success in their personal and professional lives, settle into their comfort zones, and settle for mediocrity.

Admit it, you've settled in life. You've become comfortable with a job that pays you a steady paycheck. You've become comfortable with your relationships, your skills, and your knowledge. You're just like everyone else. You've settled for mediocrity.

The problem with mediocrity is that you sacrifice your full potential and place yourself at risk of loss.

You sacrifice your full potential in personal, professional, and financial matters. You sacrifice a wealthy life when you settle for a job that pays you $50k or $100k a year. You sacrifice a life full of meaningful work when you settle for a job that you're comfortable in. You sacrifice a life full of rewarding relationships when you settle with your current circle of friends.

You risk losing everything you've gained up unto this point. You risk financial calamity if you lose your job and you risk living a life of loneliness if you fail at your relationships.

Mediocrity is a poison pill that feels good going down, but can have a devastating effect once it's ingested.

The key to guaranteed success and happiness in life is to never settle, never atrophy, never stop reaching for greater success.

Despite what others may consider to be my enormous success in my entrepreneurial ventures, I do not often feel that I am successful. I don't feel successful because I have not achieved my full potential. I'm someone who keeps trying new things, trying to do something different, something bigger, something better.

I'm never satisfied. While I may be happy, I'm not satisfied. That's because there's always something more out there to be accomplished, and greater goals for me to reach.

I've been told that I should be happy with what I have and with what I've accomplished. Without knowing it, people have told me to settle. They've tried to tell me to accept mediocrity. Fuck that.

I've made my first million dollars. I've achieved the financial success that others desire, and what my younger self aspired to. But I'm not stopping there. I'm working on becoming a billionaire before I die. Why? Because it's a bigger target - a checkmark on my bucket list of life. And once I reach the billion-dollar mark, I'll shoot for something even greater.

I have a poster in my office that reminds me to continue to strive for more when I start to get content and lazy. It's a simple poster with white text on a black background and a straightforward, simple message – *"Fuck Mediocrity"*.

If you want to achieve great success in your life, you cannot accept mediocrity. You must constantly be looking for ways to do more, be more, help more people, and accomplish greater things.

Your current circle of friends isn't likely to help you reach your greatest potential. It's not because they're bad people - it's because they're probably like you are right now. They think like you and act like you do now. If you want to achieve more, you need to think and act differently than you do now.

In order to achieve something greater, you need to listen to and learn from people that have achieved greater success than you currently have.

I don't really listen much to the people who have the same or lesser levels of success than I do. I listen to people that have greater levels of success, because that's what I want.

I listen to people like Robert Kiyosaki, Dan Lok, Dan Peña, Grant Cardone, and Richard Branson. I read books like *Think and Grow Rich*, *The Richest Man In Babylon*, *The Millionaire Fastlane*, *The Wealthy Gardener*, and *F.U. Money*.

Ask yourself - who are you listening to and where are you getting your information?

Chapter Thirty One
Make Your Wealth Last

Once you begin to generate more income with the knowledge you've found in this book, you need to start thinking about how you're going to keep that money and make it work for you.

You want to use some of that money to grow your wealth, achieve financial freedom, and ensure that you never run out of money <u>ever</u>.

I detail the methods that the wealthy use to ensure their continued riches in my book *Perpetual Wealth*.

If you want to achieve true financial wealth, you need to read that book.

In *Perpetual Wealth*, I teach you everything you've wanted to know about money that the wealthy have hid from you, including:

- The lies you've been told about money
- The mindset you need to have to become wealthy

- How to make your money work for you
- How to build "wealth machines"
- How to allocate your investments wisely
- How to diversify across multiple asset classes
- Efficient ways to make more money

If you care about your future, if you care about your children, you owe it to yourself to read *Perpetual Wealth*.

Chapter Thirty Two
Handling Success

Money Might Change You

Some people say that money changes you. That's somewhat true, but not in a bad way. In truth, money doesn't change who you are. Instead, it simply amplifies who you already are.

For example, if you like buying shoes before you become wealthy, you're likely to buy even more shoes when you're wealthy. If you're a good person before you come into money, you'll be a good person after you have money.

One thing that wealth will change in you is your ability to relax knowing that your financial future is secure. It will provide you with the things and experiences that can enrich your life. It will increase your happiness (to a point) by providing you with those things.

Having more money will (hopefully) let you appreciate life far more than those who simply work their years away by chasing their next paycheck. Once you're truly wealthy you won't need to trade your time for money. Instead, your money will be working for you. And that will allow you the freedom to spend your time doing the things in life that really matter to you.

You Might Lose Friends

You generally won't find successful people talking about this topic much. Most people don't understand what it takes to become successful and what you have to do to get there. They'll focus on the outcome, while ignoring the path that successful people had to take to achieve their wealth.

From my own experience as an entrepreneur, I went through stages where I lost friends and acquaintances due to my success. Some of the people who supported me when I was getting started became jealous and critical once I became successful.

I've talked with several other successful entrepreneurs who have experienced the same thing in their own lives. And you'll likely experience it when you become more successful too.

I believe the basic reason why this happens is envy. Everyone loves an underdog and the story of someone who's going through a struggle. But once a hero emerges, they grow envious of the fame and/or fortune that person achieves.

You shouldn't fear losing friends as your success grows. You'll find new friends and acquaintances that better align with your successful self than your old circle. That's a good thing, because your circle of friends and influencers determines your future success. If you surround yourself with good, positive people that challenge you, have high aspirations and a good work ethic, you're much more likely to succeed than if you have people around you that don't exemplify those attributes.

Chapter Thirty Three
Free Yourself From Blocks

In order to become wealthy, you're first going to have to free yourself of any blocks to wealth that might be holding you back. Without even knowing it, most of us have negative views of money and wealth pounded into our subconscious from a young age.

Before you can be effective at building your wealth, you have to examine why you want the wealth, how you're going to build it, and what obstacles might block your path in achieving it.

Let's examine some of the wealth blocks that society tries to ingrain in us...

Money Isn't All That Matters

No kidding. People that say this are often the one's who don't have as much money as they need or would like to have. It's almost used as an excuse as to why they don't have the financial resources they'd like.

It's true that your experiences and relationships in life are more important than money itself. However, money helps you have more wonderful experiences, improve your standard of living, and provide for your family. And those things do matter.

What's a valuable lesson to learn is that money doesn't matter until it does. If you or a family member are faced with a disease that could be solved by an expensive surgery, money <u>will</u> matter. If you have the money, you can have the life-saving surgery. If you don't have money, you can't. Money does matter. Big time.

Money Doesn't Bring Happiness

This saying is also parroted by people that don't have as much money as they'd like. This saying is partially true, but not in the context or manner that people use it in. The truth is that a lack of money can severely affect your happiness in life. If you don't have enough money, you can find yourself stressed through life. And that will make you unhappy.

It is true that an increase in your wealth doesn't correspond directly to your happiness. A millionaire isn't a million times happier than the person that has one dollar to their name. There is certainly a diminishing return with regards to how much happiness money can buy.

Money Doesn't Make You A Bad Person

When I was a teenager, there were a few rich kids in my school. Actually, the kids weren't rich. They were the kids of rich parents. And some of those kids were mean (or at least I thought they were). That impression led me to create a construct in my mind that equated having money to being a bad person. I had to address that issue and see that it wasn't true before I could become financially successful.

In society today, there is a growing discontent over the wealth gap. People refer to this as "wealth inequality", as if all people are supposed to share wealth equally. I for one do not feel obligated to give my wealth to those who have chosen not to save, invest, or grow their own wealth. Nor do I think it right that the government, or anyone else for that matter, should have the right to forcefully take it from me to give to others.

Still, many people hold the view that the "1 percent" in society are somehow evil and should be made to pay for everything the 99 percent want. Calls to tax the rich are heard loudly in political rallies. The rich are made out to be evil people who have taken advantage of others in order to have accumulated their wealth. Socialist ideals seem to be spreading like wildfire.

I know many people who despise the rich. And yet I don't know a single person – not a single one – who would not like to be a millionaire or multi-millionaire themselves. That's real hypocrisy in action. If you hold a negative view of wealthy people, what do you think the chances are that you will yourself become wealthy?

Money Is The Root Of All Evil

Societal beliefs about money can be strange and even downright lies. The mantra that "money is the root of all evil" is something that I believe holds people back in achieving great wealth. This is a pretty pervasive and damaging lie that we've all been told, and I destroy it in my book *Perpetual Wealth*.

Chapter Thirty Four
Don't Trade Your Life For Money

If you had a million dollars in the bank and someone held a gun to your head and offered you your life in exchange for your money, you'd take them up on that offer in a heartbeat. You inherently know that your life is worth way more than money. So why then, is it you're trading your life for money?

Most people spend their entire adult lives slaving away at a job they don't like just to pay their bills. They spend all the money they earn and fail to build savings and investments that can increase their wealth and ensure a secure retirement. Thus, they are wage slaves trapped until they die in a sadistic rat race that they never manage to escape.

A recent Gallup poll found that as much as 85 percent of people hate their jobs. That's an incredibly depressing number when you realize that a person's employment eats up their majority of their waking hours in adult life. Spending the majority of your life doing something you hate doesn't sound like a very fulfilling way to live your life.

If you're a young man or woman just starting out in your career, you might feel enthusiastic about your job and what the future holds for you. However, if you're like the vast majority of your older coworkers, you'll find that you eventually end up hating your job or switching fields altogether one or more times in your life. That means there's a good chance you'll end up working in a field that has nothing to do with your college degree or training. To top that off, chances are that you'll be receiving small pay increases over time unless you increase your skillset immensely and change jobs. How's that for an optimistic look into the future?

From a young age we're all taught to go to school, get good grades, and get a good job. That sounds good in theory. And while education is extremely valuable in life, it's what we're not taught that can really hold us back from achieving a lifetime of happiness and financial security.

Most people do the best they can in school and get the best job they can for the best pay. They focus on getting pay increases to increase their "wealth" as they progress through their career. This strategy doesn't seem to work all that well for most people, as the vast majority of the population fails to build their wealth and ensure their financial prosperity.

So what's the problem with what we've been told? There's a key element to understanding money that we're not taught by society. There's something that the wealthy understand that others don't...

Wealthy people understand that working for money isn't going to make you rich. Instead, they know that working for money keeps you poor.

At this point you're probably thinking I'm completely off base. Those statements make no sense to most people. I'll dive into that in the next chapter (of *Perpetual Wealth*).

For the time being, just understand that there's nothing wrong with having a job and earning a paycheck. It's how the vast majority of people get started obtaining their wealth. It's just not the most efficient way to go about things.

The downside to earning your money through a job is that it's time-intensive and can take away from your life in terms of time that you can't otherwise spend with your friends and family, and doing things you find more fulfilling.

While you're earning your money through your job, I think it's imperative that you take time to learn high-income skills. This can make you more valuable in the workplace and increase your pay much more substantially than would otherwise happen if you didn't learn new skills. Constant learning is a key component of life that wealthy people pursue.

Once you obtain more skills, you're able to transition to higher paying jobs. Assuming you control your spending and divert much of your new earnings to savings and investments, that increased pay can substantially improve your financial security and get you on the path to building significant wealth in your lifetime.

When you earn money through a job you're trading your time for money. The downside to that – even if you enjoy your job – is that there are only a certain amount of hours that you can work each week. Thus, there's a cap on how much you can earn. Even though you might earn a lot per hour, you can't obtain unlimited earnings potential through a job.

There are more efficient ways to earn more money than your regular job. Time efficiency is critical to building wealth, as time is limited and the more your harness its potential, the more you can succeed.

You can employ several different methods to start supplementing the earnings from your job and even potentially quit your job if you are able to succeed. I cover some of the methods for generating money efficiently near the end of the book *Perpetual Wealth*.

Section 6

-

Resources

Resources

For more information about resources, useful links, and additional books and educational material, visit the ZeroToHero.co website at:

http://zerotohero.co

On that site you'll find free videos that cover various topics including finance and personal growth.

Recommended Reading

Here are just a few of the books that I believe would be useful in your understanding of finance, wealth, and investing.   You can find all these books for sale at Amazon.com

 **Think and Grow Rich**

 **The Millionaire Next Door: The Surprising Secrets of America's Wealthy**

Recommended Reading Cont'd

The Richest Man In Babylon

The 4-Hour Work Week

Think and Grow Rich

"Think and Grow Rich" is a phenomenal book written by Napolean Hill. It's not a new book by any means, but its messages are timeless. It's been said that millionaires re-read this book on a regular basis to remind themselves about its principles.

An essential message of the book is that "ordinary" people can obtain extraordinary outcomes if they just apply themselves, taking things step by step.

The ideas in the book extend far beyond just obtaining financial wealth and business success. You can use the principals to grow rich in compassion, courage, and abilities as well. If you don't want to take the time to read the book, you can watch the "Think And Grow Rich: The Legacy" movie on Amazon.com to get a synopsis of some of the book's core concepts.

I can't say enough about this book!

Zero To Hero Website

The official Zero To Hero website is online at:

http://zerotohero.co

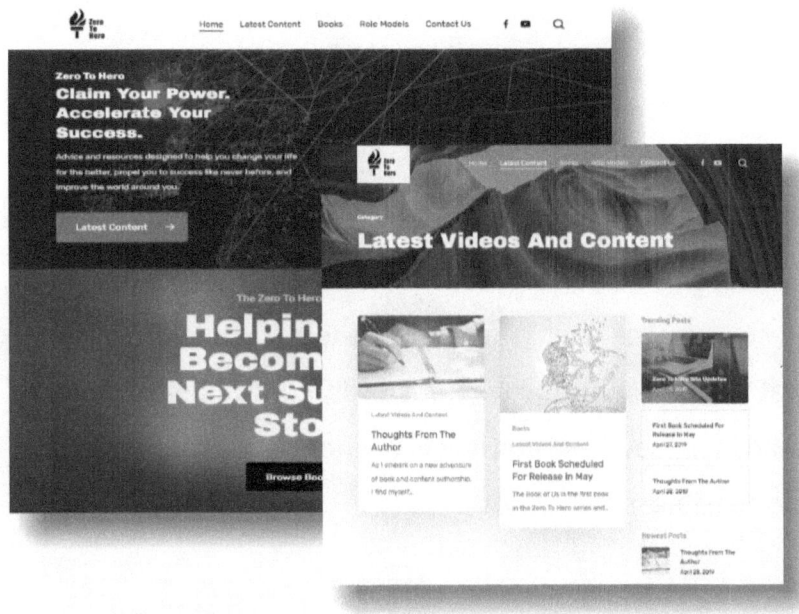

The website contains information on the latest book releases and features original videos that cover topics on finance, personal growth, inspirational stories, and ideas for improving our world.

Have a question about the book or have an idea for a new video? Use the contact page on the website to get in touch with me. I'd love to hear from you!

Inspiring Role Models

I'm inspired by many people (and many companies) and I consider them all to be role models for different reasons. I've put together a list of these people and companies on the Zero To Hero website at:

http://zerotohero.co/role-models

Below you'll find a short list of some of the people that inspire me and why. I would encourage you to write down your own list and see who inspires you. Follow their lead in your personal path to self-improvement and financial betterment, and you can achieve greater levels of success than you ever thought possible.

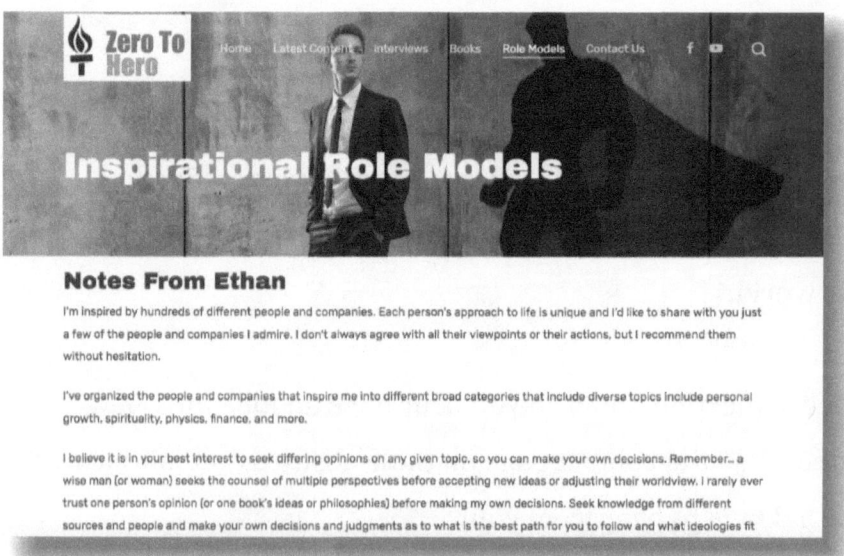

I'm inspired by:

My son.
His constant quest for learning reminds me of my childhood and inspires me to be the best father I can be.

My fiancé.
Her unwavering love and support have helped me get through many tough times.

The friends I have.
They support me in times of need and challenge me to grow.

The friends I've lost.
They forced me to look inside myself to see where I had to grow.

My parents.
Their dedication to teaching and caring for my sister and me will never be forgotten.

My doubters and competitors.
They help me to push forward harder. The race would be much less fun without them.

My team at Nagios.
Everyone in the company (present and past) has taught me so much. Thanks team!

Jeff Bezos.
For his vision and dedication into building Amazon.com into the powerful company that provides so many of us with an easier life. I'm especially grateful for the ease at which an independent-minded person such as myself can self-publish a book without searching for a publisher who believes in my ideas.

Elon Musk.
For his tenacity and dedication to building SpaceX and Tesla, while continually proving that you can overcome the doubters and achieve great heights. I love what you do and so do many others. After all, what young kid doesn't like rockets?

Richard Branson.
For building his empire of companies from its early humble beginnings as a record store.

Michael Dell.
For starting a well-respected technology company from his dorm room in college.

Warren Buffet.
For his phenomenal success and upbeat attitude that started from hard work and humble beginnings.

Bill Gates and **Steve Jobs**.
For building two amazing companies that have changed the world of computing forever.

The team at Hewlett-Packard.
For creating amazing technology solutions and an awesome *"Make It Matter"* video that is truly inspiring and perhaps the best company promo video I've ever seen.

The team at Goalcast...
Jay Shetty...
Tom Bilyeu of **Impact Theory...**
Nuseir Yassin of **NAS Daily...**
and **Prince EA**...
For providing inspiring messages that promote growth, understanding, and self-improvement.

Jim Kwik.
For his explanation of how our brains work and how we can unlock our full potential.

"Rich Dad" Robert Kiyosaki.
For teaching me the value of financial concepts and the importance of cash-flowing assets.

Mike Maloney of **GoldSilver.com**.
For his dedication to education people about the financial world.

Dan Peña (the 50 billion dollar man).
For his enormous successes and his continued dedication to teaching others his methods. And for the fact that he swears like me.

Dan Lok.
For his business and financial success and his dedication to teach.

Mark Moss from **Market Disruptors**.
For presenting complex ideas in a straightforward, humble, and no-nonsense manner.

William Hurley (whurley).
For providing me with inspiration as to what one person with dedication can accomplish. I admire you, my friend!

Alex Koffmann.
For being one of the best friends I could ask for. You've saved my ass more than once buddy!